AI N.L.P.
PROMPT PRACTITIONER

CLASS TEXTBOOK

BY: DR. JOSEPH G. MUCHA, J.D.
A.I. PROMPT DOCTOR

**PRACTITIONER DEGREE
CLASS TEXTBOOK**

TABLE OF CONTENTS

CHAPTER 1
INTRODUCTION TO A.I. N.L.P.
PROMPT PRACTITIONER

This course is the starting point for your journey in mastering the art of using A.I. N.L.P. to generate text.

The A.I. N.L.P. Prompt Practitioner Textbook is designed to provide you with a comprehensive understanding of the fundamentals of using A.I. N.L.P. for generating high-quality text.

Throughout the course, you will learn how to formulate clear and conzcise prompts, understand the workings of the A.I. N.L.P. model, and generate text that is coherent and relevant to your task.

Our course will be structured around four main themes, each corresponding to the different levels of expertise in our Prompt Degree Program. These themes are: Practitioner, Engineer, Master, and Doctor.

In this introductory course, we will be focusing on the Practitioner level, where you will learn the foundational concepts of prompt formulation, data preprocessing, model training, and output generation.

By the end of the course, you will have developed the skills and knowledge necessary to create compelling prompts and generate coherent and relevant text outputs.

You will also learn how to evaluate the quality of generated text and make improvements to your models based on feedback.

In this course, you will learn the basics of prompt formulation, data preprocessing, model training, and output generation.

You will also learn how to evaluate the quality of generated text and make improvements to your models based on feedback.

Here is a breakdown of some of the topics that will be covered in the Prompt Practitioner Textbook:

Introduction to ChatGPT:
You will learn the basics of what A.I. N.L.P. is, how it works, and how it differs from other NLP models.

Prompt Formulation:
You will learn how to formulate clear and concise prompts that are appropriate for your task.

Data Preprocessing:
You will learn how to prepare your data for use in ChatGPT, including techniques for cleaning and formatting text data.

Model Training:
You will learn how to train your A.I. N.L.P. model using the provided data and how to fine-tune the mode.

Output Generation:
You will learn how to generate text outputs based on your prompts for post-processing and filtering the generated text.

Quality Evaluation:
You will learn how to evaluate the quality of your generated text using metrics such as perplexity and human evaluation.

Throughout the course, you will have the opportunity to practice your skills by completing hands-on exercises and projects at home. By the end of the course, you will have a solid understanding of the fundamentals of using A.I. N.L.P. for generating text, and you will be well on your way to becoming a A.I. N.L.P. expert.

We are excited to embark on this journey with you and look forward to guiding you in your quest to become a A.I. N.L.P. Prompt expert. Let's get started!

What Is A.I. N.L.P. And Its Applications

A.I. N.L.P. is a state-of-the-art deep learning model that is capable of generating human-like text responses based on a given prompt.

Developed by OpenAI, A.I. N.L.P. is a generative language model that uses unsupervised learning techniques to understand the patterns and structure of human language.

It has been trained on massive amounts of text data, allowing it to generate coherent and contextually relevant responses to a wide range of prompts.

One of the key applications of A.I. N.L.P. is in the field of conversational AI. With its ability to generate human-like responses, A.I. N.L.P. can be used to create chatbots and virtual assistants that can interact with humans in a natural and intuitive manner.

This technology has significant implications for businesses, as it can improve customer service and automate routine tasks.

Another important application of A.I. N.L.P. is in content creation. With the ability to generate high-quality text based on a given prompt, A.I. N.L.P. can be used to create articles, stories, and other written content.

This technology has the potential to revolutionize content creation, as it can save time and effort while maintaining high standards of quality.

A.I. N.L.P. can also be used in a wide range of other applications, such as language translation, sentiment analysis, and text summarization.

With its versatility and flexibility, A.I. N.L.P. is quickly becoming a crucial tool in the field of NLP.

A.I. N.L.P. is a cutting-edge language model that has the potential to transform numerous industries and applications.

Its ability to generate human-like text based on a given prompt makes it an incredibly valuable tool for conversational AI, content creation, and other NLP applications.

As the technology continues to evolve, we can expect to see even more innovative uses for A.I. N.L.P. in the future.

Understanding the Prompt-Response Basics

Let's introduce you to the basics of understanding the prompt-response process in ChatGPT.

To begin, it is essential to understand that the prompt is the input that you provide to the A.I. N.L.P. model. It is the text that you want the model to generate a response for. The response, on the other hand, is the output generated by the model in response to the prompt.

The goal of the prompt-response process is to generate high-quality text that is coherent and relevant to the given prompt. To achieve this goal, it is crucial to pay attention to the following key factors:

Clarity Of The Prompt:

The prompt should be clear and specific, with a well-defined objective. It should be concise and unambiguous to avoid any confusion or misinterpretation by the model.

Appropriateness Of The Prompt:

The prompt should be appropriate for the task at hand. It should be relevant to the desired output and should contain all the necessary information that the model needs to generate a high-quality response.

Quality Of The Response:

The response generated by the model should be coherent, contextually relevant, and grammatically correct. It should also be consistent with the desired output.

Relevance Of The Response:

The response generated by the model should be relevant to the prompt. It should be focused on the objective of the prompt and should avoid any irrelevant or extraneous information.

In order to achieve these factors, it is important to carefully design and formulate your prompts, ensuring that they are clear, appropriate, and focused.

Additionally, it is important to evaluate the quality of the generated text and make improvements to the model as necessary.

By mastering the basics of prompt-response in ChatGPT, you will be well on your way to creating high-quality, relevant, and coherent text outputs that can be used in a wide range of applications.

Let's dive a bit deeper into each of these key factors to gain a better understanding of how to optimize the prompt-response process in ChatGPT.

Clarity Of The Prompt:

The prompt should be clear and specific, with a well-defined objective. This means that it should be free of any ambiguity, vagueness, or unnecessary complexity that may confuse the model.

One effective way to ensure clarity is to use simple, concise language that is easy for the model to understand. Additionally, the prompt should be tailored to the desired output and should include any necessary context or background information.

Appropriateness Of The Prompt:

The prompt should be appropriate for the task at hand. This means that it should be relevant to the desired output and should contain all the necessary information that the model needs to generate a high-quality response.

It is important to consider the intended audience and purpose of the generated text when formulating the prompt.

For example, if the output is intended for a general audience, the prompt should be written in simple, accessible language.

Quality Of The Response:

The response generated by the model should be coherent, contextually relevant, and grammatically correct. This means that it should be well-structured, with a logical flow and clear connections between ideas.

Additionally, it should be appropriate for the context and should avoid any irrelevant or extraneous information. It is important to carefully evaluate the quality of the response and make improvements to the model as necessary.

Relevance Of The Response:

The response generated by the model should be relevant to the prompt. This means that it should be focused on the objective of the prompt and should avoid any irrelevant or extraneous information. It is important to carefully consider the intended audience and purpose of the generated text when evaluating the relevance of the response.

By paying close attention to these key factors, you can optimize the prompt-response process in A.I. N.L.P. to generate high-quality, relevant, and coherent text outputs.

With practice and experience, you can develop your skills in prompt formulation and model training to become an expert in using A.I. N.L.P. for text generation.

How to Generate Text Using ChatGPT

Generating text using A.I. N.L.P. involves several key steps. Let's walk through them together:

Step 1: Choose Your Prompt

The first step in generating text using A.I. N.L.P. is to choose your prompt. This is the text that you want the model to generate a response for. It should be clear, specific, and tailored to the desired output.

Step 2: Fine-Tune The Model

Once you have your prompt, you need to fine-tune the A.I. N.L.P. model to generate the desired output. Fine-tuning involves training the model on a specific task or dataset to optimize its ability to generate relevant, high-quality text outputs.

Step 3: Generate the response

With your prompt and fine-tuned model in place, you can generate the response. Simply input your prompt into the model and allow it to generate the corresponding text output.

Step 4: Evaluate the response

Once the response is generated, it is important to carefully evaluate it for quality, coherence, and relevance. This involves assessing the structure, grammar, and content of the generated text to ensure that it meets the intended objective and is suitable for the intended audience.

Step 5: Refine the model

Based on the evaluation of the generated text, you may need to refine the model to optimize its ability to generate high-quality, relevant text outputs. This can involve adjusting the training dataset, fine-tuning the model parameters, or experimenting with different input/output formats.

Step 6: Iterate

Generating high-quality text using A.I. N.L.P. is an iterative process. It requires ongoing experimentation, evaluation, and refinement to optimize the model's ability to generate coherent, relevant text outputs. By continually iterating on the process and refining the model, you can achieve optimal results and generate text outputs that meet your specific needs and objectives.

Generating text using A.I. N.L.P. involves choosing a clear, specific prompt, fine-tuning the model, generating the response, evaluating the response, refining the model, and iterating on the process.

Let's dive a bit deeper into each of these steps to gain a better understanding of how to generate text using ChatGPT.

Step 1: Choose your prompt

Choosing a clear and specific prompt is key to generating high-quality text using ChatGPT. The prompt should be tailored to the desired output and should provide all the necessary information that the model needs to generate a relevant response.

One effective way to ensure clarity is to use simple, concise language that is easy for the model to understand. Additionally, the prompt should be free of any ambiguity, vagueness, or unnecessary complexity that may confuse the model.

Step 2: Fine-tune the model

Fine-tuning the A.I. N.L.P. model involves training it on a specific task or dataset to optimize its ability to generate relevant, high-quality text outputs. This can involve adjusting the model's hyperparameters, such as the number of layers or nodes, and fine-tuning its weights based on the desired output.

It is important to carefully evaluate the performance of the model during this process and make adjustments as necessary.

Step 3: Generate the response

Generating the response involves inputting the prompt into the fine-tuned model and allowing it to generate the corresponding text output. It is important to carefully evaluate the output for coherence, grammar, and relevance to the prompt.

Step 4: Evaluate The Response

Evaluating the generated response is a crucial step in the text generation process. It involves assessing the quality, coherence, and relevance of the generated text to ensure that it meets the intended objective and is suitable for the intended audience. This may involve manual evaluation by a human expert or automated evaluation using metrics such as perplexity or BLEU score.

Step 5: Refine the model

Based on the evaluation of the generated response, you may need to refine the model to optimize its ability to generate high-quality, relevant text outputs. This can involve adjusting the training dataset, fine-tuning the model parameters, or experimenting with different input/output formats.

Generating high-quality text using A.I. N.L.P. is an iterative process. It requires ongoing experimentation, evaluation, and refinement to optimize the model's ability to generate coherent, relevant text outputs.

By continually iterating on the process and refining the model, you can achieve optimal results and generate text outputs that meet your specific needs and objectives.

As stated, generating text using A.I. N.L.P. involves choosing a clear and specific prompt, fine-tuning the model, generating the response, evaluating the response, refining the model, and iterating on the process.

With practice and experience, you can become an expert in using A.I. N.L.P. to generate high-quality, relevant, and coherent text outputs.

CHAPTER 2:
NATURAL LANGUAGE PROCESSING
BASICS

Chapter 2 of the ChatGPT Prompt Practitioner Textbook is focused on natural language processing (NLP) basics. This chapter is designed to provide students with a foundational understanding of the key concepts and techniques used in NLP, which will serve as a critical framework for their understanding of ChatGPT and its applications.

The chapter covers a range of topics, including:

Introduction To NLP:

The chapter begins with an overview of NLP, including its key applications and challenges. Students will learn about the various approaches to NLP, including rule-based, statistical, and machine learning-based methods.

Text Preprocessing:

Text preprocessing is an essential step in NLP, and this chapter covers the key techniques involved in preparing text data for analysis. Students will learn about tokenization, stop word removal, stemming, and lemmatization, and how these techniques can be used to enhance the accuracy and effectiveness of NLP models.

Text Representation:

The chapter also covers the various approaches to representing text data in NLP, including bag-of-words models, term frequency-inverse document frequency (TF-IDF) models, and word embeddings. Students will learn about the strengths and weaknesses of each approach and how they can be used to optimize the performance of NLP models.

Language Modeling:

Language modeling is a critical component of NLP, and this chapter provides an overview of the key concepts and techniques involved in modeling language. Students will learn about n-grams, Markov models, and neural language models, and how they can be used to generate coherent and relevant text outputs.

Evaluation Metrics:
Finally, the chapter covers the various evaluation metrics used in NLP to assess the performance of models. Students will learn about metrics such as precision, recall, F1-score, and accuracy, and how they can be used to evaluate the effectiveness of NLP models.

Chapter 2 provides students with a solid foundation in the key concepts and techniques used in NLP, which will serve as a critical framework for their understanding of ChatGPT and its applications.

Here are some additional details about each section of Chapter 2:

Introduction to NLP:
This section provides an overview of NLP and its applications, including sentiment analysis, text classification, named entity recognition, and machine translation. Students will also learn about the challenges of NLP, such as ambiguity, context sensitivity, and data sparsity.

Text Preprocessing:
Text preprocessing involves cleaning and transforming raw text data into a format that can be analyzed by NLP models.

This section covers key techniques such as tokenization (splitting text into individual words or tokens), stop word removal (eliminating common words that do not carry much meaning), stemming (reducing words to their base or root form), and lemmatization (similar to stemming, but more precise).

Text Representation:
Once text has been preprocessed, it must be represented in a way that can be analyzed by NLP models. This section covers different approaches to text representation, such as bag-of-words models (representing text as a collection of unique words),

TF-IDF models (giving more weight to words that are rare in a given corpus), and word embeddings (representing words as dense vectors in a high-dimensional space).

Language Modeling:
Language modeling is the process of predicting the likelihood of a sequence of words occurring in a given context.

This section covers different language modeling techniques, such as n-grams (predicting the probability of a word based on its preceding n-1 words), Markov models (predicting the probability of a word based on its immediate predecessor), and neural language models (using deep learning techniques to model complex relationships between words and context).

Evaluation Metrics:
To assess the performance of NLP models, various evaluation metrics can be used. This section covers key metrics such as precision (the proportion of true positives among all predicted positives), recall (the proportion of true positives among all actual positives), F1-score (a weighted average of precision and recall), and accuracy (the proportion of correctly classified instances).

Students will also learn about the importance of selecting appropriate evaluation metrics based on the specific task and objectives of the NLP model.

By the end of Chapter 2, students will have a solid understanding of the key concepts and techniques used in NLP, which will serve as a foundation for their future work with ChatGPT and other NLP tools and models.

Introduction to
Natural Language Processing (NLP)

Introduction to Natural Language Processing (NLP) is a critical concept in the field of artificial intelligence and computer science. NLP involves the study of how computers can process and understand natural language text or speech in order to extract meaning and perform various tasks.

NLP is used in a wide range of applications, from chatbots and virtual assistants to language translation and sentiment analysis. NLP models can be used to analyze and interpret large volumes of unstructured text data, such as social media posts, customer reviews, and news articles.

There are several key challenges in NLP, including ambiguity, context sensitivity, and data sparsity. Natural language is often ambiguous, and the meaning of a given sentence can vary depending on the context in which it is used.

For example, the word "bank" can refer to a financial institution or the side of a river. NLP models must be able to understand and disambiguate such words in order to accurately interpret text.

Context sensitivity is another challenge in NLP. The meaning of a word or phrase can change depending on the broader context in which it is used.

For example, the word "run" can refer to physical activity or to operating a computer program. NLP models must be able to recognize and interpret these contextual nuances in order to accurately analyze text.

Data sparsity is a challenge in NLP due to the vast amount of possible combinations of words and phrases in natural language. NLP models must be able to effectively learn from limited amounts of data and generalize to new or unseen text data.

In order to overcome these challenges, NLP researchers and practitioners use a range of techniques and approaches, including machine learning, deep learning, and linguistic analysis.

These techniques are used to build models that can analyze and interpret natural language text with increasing accuracy and precision.

NLP is a critical area of research and development in the field of artificial intelligence and has enormous potential to transform how we interact with computers and process large volumes of text data.

Here are some additional details about NLP and its applications:

NLP involves the use of computational techniques to analyze and interpret natural language text. Some of the tasks that can be performed using NLP include:

Sentiment Analysis:
This involves analyzing text data to determine the sentiment or emotional tone of the text. Sentiment analysis can be used to analyze customer feedback, social media posts, and other text data to understand how people feel about a particular product or service.

Named Entity Recognition:
This involves identifying and extracting specific entities from text data, such as people, organizations, locations, and dates. Named entity recognition can be used in various applications, such as information extraction and text summarization.

Text Classification:
This involves classifying text data into predefined categories, such as spam vs. non-spam emails or positive vs. negative reviews. Text classification can be used in various applications, such as content filtering and recommendation systems.

Machine Translation:
This involves translating text from one language to another. Machine translation is used in various applications, such as online translation services and multilingual chatbots.

To perform these tasks, A.I. N.L.P. models use various techniques and approaches, such as:

> Tokenization:
> This involves breaking text into individual tokens or words.
>
> Lemmatization And Stemming:
> These techniques involve reducing words to their base or root form, which can help to reduce the dimensionality of text data and improve model performance.
>
> Part-Of-Speech Tagging:
> This involves labeling words in text data with their corresponding part of speech, such as noun, verb, or adjective.
>
> Dependency Parsing:
> This involves analyzing the grammatical structure of sentences to identify the relationships between words.
>
> Word Embeddings:
> This involves representing words as dense vectors in a high-dimensional space, which can capture semantic relationships between words.

Overall, NLP is a rapidly evolving field with many exciting applications and opportunities for research and development. By understanding the basics of NLP, students can gain a solid foundation for working with ChatGPT and other NLP models and tools.

One of the most important applications of NLP is in the field of chatbots and virtual assistants. Chatbots are computer programs that can simulate conversations with human users using natural language.

Chatbots can be used in a wide range of applications, such as customer service, personal assistance, and language learning.

To build effective chatbots, NLP models must be able to understand and interpret natural language text input and generate appropriate responses.

Chatbots use various techniques and approaches, such as:

Intent recognition:
This involves identifying the intent or purpose behind a user's input, such as requesting information or making a reservation.

Dialogue Management:
This involves managing the flow of the conversation and generating appropriate responses based on the user's input.

Natural Language Generation:
This involves generating natural language responses that are appropriate and relevant to the user's input.

Another important application of NLP is in the field of information extraction and text analytics. NLP models can be used to automatically extract structured information from unstructured text data, such as news articles or social media posts.

This information can be used to identify trends and patterns, monitor brand reputation, and perform various other analyses.

NLP can also be used in the field of language translation. Machine translation involves using NLP models to automatically translate text from one language to another.

This can be useful in a wide range of applications, such as international business, language learning, and cross-cultural communication.

NLP can be used in the field of sentiment analysis. Sentiment analysis involves using NLP models to analyze text data and determine the sentiment or emotional tone of the text.

This can be useful in applications such as social media monitoring, customer feedback analysis, and brand reputation management.

NLP is a rapidly evolving field with many exciting applications and opportunities for research and development. By understanding the basics of NLP and its applications, students can gain a solid foundation for working with ChatGPT and other NLP models and tools.

Parts of Speech (POS) Tagging

Parts of speech (POS) tagging is a fundamental task in natural language processing (NLP) that involves labeling each word in a text with its corresponding part of speech, such as noun, verb, adjective, or adverb.

POS tagging can be used in various NLP applications, such as text classification, named entity recognition, and machine translation.

POS tagging is a challenging task because many words can function as multiple parts of speech depending on the context in which they are used. For example, the word "run" can be a noun ("I went for a run"), a verb ("I run every morning"), or an adjective ("She has a run in her stockings").

To perform POS tagging, NLP models use various techniques and approaches, such as:

Rule-Based Methods: These methods use a set of rules or patterns to assign POS tags to words. Rule-based methods can be effective in some cases, but they are limited by the number and complexity of rules that can be defined.

Dictionary-Based Methods: These methods use a pre-defined dictionary or lexicon that associates each word with its most common part of speech.

Dictionary-based methods can be effective for many common words, but they may not work well for less common or specialized words.

Machine Learning-Based Methods: These methods use statistical models that are trained on large datasets of annotated text. Machine learning-based methods can be highly effective and flexible, but they require large amounts of annotated data for training.

Overall, POS tagging is a critical task in NLP that enables various downstream applications. By understanding the basics of POS tagging and its techniques, students can gain a solid foundation for working with ChatGPT and other NLP models and tools. Here are some additional details about POS tagging:

POS tagging is based on the idea that each word in a text can be classified into one of several categories based on its syntactic and semantic properties. The most common categories include:

Noun: A word that represents a person, place, thing, or idea (e.g., "dog", "city", "love").

Verb: A word that represents an action or state of being (e.g., "run", "think", "is").

Adjective: A word that describes a noun or pronoun (e.g., "red", "happy", "tall").

Adverb: A word that describes a verb, adjective, or other adverb (e.g., "quickly", "very", "quite").

Pronoun: A word that replaces a noun or noun phrase (e.g., "he", "she", "they").

Preposition: A word that shows the relationship between a noun or pronoun and other words in a sentence (e.g., "in", "on", "under").

Conjunction: A word that connects words, phrases, or clauses (e.g., "and", "but", "or").

Interjection: A word that expresses strong emotions or feelings (e.g., "wow", "ouch", "oh").

POS tagging can be performed at various levels of granularity, such as at the word, sentence, or document level.

For example, a POS tagger might label each word in a sentence with its corresponding part of speech, or it might label each sentence in a document with its overall sentiment.

POS tagging is a critical task in many NLP applications, such as:

Text Classification: POS tags can be used as features in machine learning models that classify text into different categories, such as spam versus non-spam emails or positive versus negative reviews.

Named Entity Recognition: POS tags can be used to identify named entities, such as people, places, and organizations, in text data.

Machine Translation: POS tags can be used to improve the accuracy of machine translation by helping to disambiguate words that have multiple possible translations.

POS tagging is a fundamental task in NLP that enables various downstream applications. By understanding the basics of POS tagging and its applications, students can gain a solid foundation for working with ChatGPT and other NLP models and tools.

Text Cleaning and
Pre-Processing

Text cleaning and pre-processing are critical steps in natural language processing (NLP) that involve transforming raw text data into a format that can be analyzed by machine learning models and other NLP tools.

Text cleaning and pre-processing can help improve the quality and accuracy of NLP applications, such as sentiment analysis, text classification, and machine translation.

Here are some common techniques used in text cleaning and pre-processing:

Tokenization:

Tokenization involves breaking down a piece of text into its individual words or tokens. Tokenization is a crucial first step in many NLP applications, as it enables machines to understand the structure of the text.

Stopword Removal:

Stopwords are common words that do not carry much meaning on their own, such as "the," "a," and "an." Stopword removal involves removing these words from the text, as they can add noise to the analysis and make it harder to identify meaningful patterns.

Lowercasing:

Lowercasing involves converting all text to lowercase, which can help improve the accuracy of some NLP models, as it reduces the number of different tokens that need to be considered.

Stemming And Lemmatization:

Stemming and lemmatization are techniques used to reduce words to their base form. Stemming involves removing the suffixes from words (e.g., "run," "running," "runner" all become "run"), while lemmatization involves reducing words to their dictionary form (e.g., "goes" becomes "go").

Removing Special Characters And Numbers:
Special characters and numbers can add noise to the text and make it harder to identify meaningful patterns. Removing these elements can help improve the quality and accuracy of NLP models.

By performing these and other text cleaning and pre-processing techniques, NLP practitioners can help improve the quality and accuracy of NLP models and tools.

The goal of text cleaning and pre-processing is to create a clean and structured dataset that can be used to train and evaluate NLP models.

Here are some additional text cleaning and pre-processing techniques that can be used in NLP:

Spell Checking:
Spell checking involves identifying and correcting spelling errors in the text. This can be important, as misspelled words can alter the meaning of a sentence and make it harder for machines to understand.

Handling Contractions:
Contractions are words that are shortened by combining two words together, such as "don't" for "do not" or "can't" for "cannot." It is important to handle contractions properly during text pre-processing, as they can affect the accuracy of NLP models.

Handling Abbreviations:
Abbreviations, such as "U.S." or "Mr.," can be difficult for machines to understand. Text pre-processing techniques can be used to expand abbreviations into their full forms to make it easier for machines to interpret.

Text cleaning and pre-processing is an important step in NLP, as it can greatly impact the accuracy and performance of NLP models.

By using a combination of these techniques, NLP practitioners can create high-quality datasets that can be used to train and evaluate a variety of NLP applications.

Here are a few more advanced techniques that are commonly used in text cleaning and pre-processing:

Named Entity Recognition (N.E.R.):
Named Entity Recognition is a technique used to identify and classify named entities in text, such as people, organizations, and locations. NER can help improve the accuracy of NLP models by providing additional context to the analysis.

Part-of-Speech (POS) Tagging:
POS tagging is a technique used to identify the part of speech of each word in a sentence, such as noun, verb, adjective, etc. POS tagging can help provide additional context to the analysis and improve the accuracy of NLP models.

Dependency Parsing:
Dependency parsing is a technique used to identify the relationships between words in a sentence. It can help identify the subject, object, and verb in a sentence and provide additional context to the analysis.

Word Embeddings:
Word embeddings are a way of representing words as vectors in a high-dimensional space. Word embeddings can be used to capture semantic relationships between words, such as similarity or analogy. They are often used as input to NLP models to help improve their accuracy.

Text Augmentation:
Text augmentation involves generating new text data by applying various transformations to the existing text. For example, text augmentation can involve replacing words with synonyms, changing the word order, or inserting new sentences.

Text augmentation can help improve the quality and quantity of training data for NLP models.

By applying these advanced text cleaning and pre-processing techniques, NLP practitioners can create high-quality datasets that can be used to train and evaluate advanced NLP models.

These techniques can help improve the accuracy and performance of NLP models and enable the development of more sophisticated NLP applications.

CHAPTER 3: FINE-TUNING A.I. N.L.P.
FOR TEXT GENERATION

In this chapter, we will discuss how to fine-tune the ChatGPT model for text generation.

Fine-tuning is the process of adapting a pre-trained model to a specific task by training it on a new dataset. In the case of ChatGPT, fine-tuning involves training the model to generate text in response to a given prompt.

Here are the steps involved in fine-tuning ChatGPT for text generation:

Choose A Pre-Trained ChatGPT Model:

There are several pre-trained ChatGPT models available, such as GPT-2, GPT-3, etc. Choose a model that is appropriate for your use case based on factors such as the size of the model, the amount of training data available, and the computational resources required.

Prepare The Training Data:

The training data should consist of a collection of prompts and their corresponding responses. The quality of the training data is critical to the success of the fine-tuning process, so it is important to ensure that the data is clean, well-formatted, and diverse.

Tokenize The Training Data:

Tokenization is the process of splitting text into individual tokens, such as words or subwords. This is necessary because ChatGPT models operate at the token level rather than the character level. The tokenization process may involve using a pre-trained tokenizer or training a custom tokenizer on the training data.

Fine-Tune The Model:

Fine-tuning involves training the pre-trained ChatGPT model on the training data using techniques such as backpropagation and gradient descent. The objective is to minimize the difference between the predicted output and the actual output.

Evaluate the model:
Once the model has been trained, it is important to evaluate its performance on a held-out validation set. This involves measuring metrics such as perplexity, which is a measure of how well the model predicts the next token in a sequence.

Generate text:
Finally, the fine-tuned ChatGPT model can be used to generate text in response to a given prompt. This can be done by feeding the prompt into the model and sampling from the predicted distribution of the next token until a desired length or stopping criterion is reached.

Fine-tuning ChatGPT for text generation is a powerful technique that can be used to generate high-quality, human-like responses to prompts.

By following the steps outlined above, NLP practitioners can fine-tune ChatGPT for a wide range of text generation applications.

Here are some additional details on the fine-tuning process for ChatGPT:

Choose A Pre-Trained Chatgpt Model:

The choice of pre-trained model will depend on the specific use case and available resources. For example, the smaller GPT-2 models may be sufficient for simpler tasks, while larger models like GPT-3 may be necessary for more complex tasks. It is also important to consider the computational resources required to train and use the model, as larger models may require more powerful hardware.

Prepare The Training Data:

The quality of the training data is critical to the success of the fine-tuning process. It is important to ensure that the data is diverse and representative of the type of text that the model will be generating. Additionally, the data should be pre-processed to remove any irrelevant or noisy content, such as HTML tags or special characters.

Tokenize The Training Data:

Tokenization is the process of breaking text into smaller units, such as words or subwords. This step is necessary because ChatGPT models operate at the token level, rather than the character level. Tokenization can be done using a pre-trained tokenizer, such as the one provided with the Hugging Face Transformers library, or by training a custom tokenizer on the training data.

Fine-Tune The Model:

Fine-tuning involves training the pre-trained ChatGPT model on the training data using backpropagation and gradient descent. The objective is to minimize the difference between the predicted output and the actual output. During training, the model's parameters are updated to improve its ability to generate text in response to a given prompt.

Evaluate The Model:

Once the model has been trained, it is important to evaluate its performance on a held-out validation set. This involves measuring metrics such as perplexity, which is a measure of how well the model predicts the next token in a sequence. Other metrics that can be used to evaluate the model include BLEU score, ROUGE score, and human evaluation.

Generate Text:
Once the model has been fine-tuned and evaluated, it can be used to generate text in response to a given prompt. This is done by feeding the prompt into the model and sampling from the predicted distribution of the next token until a desired length or stopping criterion is reached.

The quality of the generated text will depend on the quality of the training data, the choice of pre-trained model, and the fine-tuning process.

Fine-tuning ChatGPT for text generation is a powerful technique that can be used to generate high-quality, human-like responses to prompts.

By following best practices in data preparation, tokenization, model selection, and evaluation, NLP practitioners can fine-tune ChatGPT for a wide range of text generation applications.

Understanding The Fine-Tuning Process

Fine-tuning is the process of adapting a pre-trained language model to a specific task by further training it on a task-specific dataset. The idea is to leverage the pre-existing knowledge of the model and fine-tune it to better understand the nuances of the task at hand. Fine-tuning ChatGPT involves several key steps:

Choosing A Pre-Trained Model:

The first step in the fine-tuning process is to choose a pre-trained ChatGPT model that is appropriate for the task at hand. The choice of model will depend on factors such as the size of the dataset, the complexity of the task, and the computational resources available.

Preparing The Dataset:

Once a pre-trained model has been selected, the next step is to prepare the dataset. This involves collecting and cleaning data that is relevant to the task. For example, if the task is to generate product descriptions, the dataset would consist of product names, features, and descriptions. The data should be pre-processed to remove any noise, irrelevant content, or special characters.

Tokenizing The Dataset:

The next step is to tokenize the dataset into individual tokens or subwords. Tokenization is the process of breaking text into smaller units that the model can understand. This step is necessary because ChatGPT operates at the token level, rather than the character level.

Fine-Tuning The Model:

Once the dataset has been tokenized, the next step is to fine-tune the model. This involves training the pre-trained ChatGPT model on the dataset using backpropagation and gradient descent.

The objective is to minimize the difference between the predicted output and the actual output. During training, the model's parameters are updated to improve its ability to generate text in response to a given prompt.

Evaluating The Model:

After the model has been fine-tuned, it is important to evaluate its performance on a held-out validation set.

This involves measuring metrics such as perplexity, which is a measure of how well the model predicts the next token in a sequence. Other metrics that can be used to evaluate the model include BLEU score, ROUGE score, and human evaluation.

Generating Text:

Once the model has been fine-tuned and evaluated, it can be used to generate text in response to a given prompt.

This is done by feeding the prompt into the model and sampling from the predicted distribution of the next token until a desired length or stopping criterion is reached.

The fine-tuning process for ChatGPT is a powerful technique that can be used to generate high-quality, human-like responses to prompts.

By following best practices in data preparation, tokenization, model selection, and evaluation, NLP practitioners can fine-tune ChatGPT for a wide range of text generation applications.

Here are some additional details on the fine-tuning process for ChatGPT:

Choosing A Pre-Trained Model:
When selecting a pre-trained ChatGPT model, it is important to consider factors such as the size of the model, the type of training data it was trained on, and the language it was trained to model.

Smaller models may be faster to fine-tune, but may not be as effective for more complex tasks. Models that were trained on similar tasks or domains may also be better suited for fine-tuning than models trained on unrelated tasks.

Preparing The Dataset:
Before fine-tuning the model, it is important to carefully prepare the dataset. This includes cleaning the data to remove any irrelevant or low-quality content, as well as splitting the data into training, validation, and test sets. It may also involve data augmentation techniques such as data synthesis or data sampling to increase the size and diversity of the dataset.

Tokenizing The Dataset:
The process of tokenization involves breaking up the text into individual tokens, such as words, subwords, or characters. This is important because ChatGPT operates at the token level, and the model can only generate text based on the tokens it has seen during training.

There are several tokenization techniques available, including byte-pair encoding (BPE), WordPiece, and sentencepiece.

Fine-Tuning The Model:
Fine-tuning involves training the pre-trained ChatGPT model on the task-specific dataset.

This typically involves several epochs of training using backpropagation and gradient descent. During training, the model's parameters are updated to minimize the difference between the predicted output and the actual output.

Hyperparameters such as the learning rate, batch size, and number of training epochs can have a significant impact on the performance of the fine-tuned model.

Evaluating The Model:

Once the model has been fine-tuned, it is important to evaluate its performance on a held-out validation set. This helps to identify any issues with overfitting or underfitting, as well as provide a measure of the model's accuracy and ability to generate coherent and relevant text.

Evaluation metrics such as perplexity, BLEU score, and ROUGE score can be used to assess the quality of the generated text.

Generating Text:

Once the model has been fine-tuned and evaluated, it can be used to generate text in response to a given prompt. This typically involves providing the model with a prompt or starting sentence, and then sampling from the predicted distribution of the next token until a desired length or stopping criterion is reached.

Techniques such as top-k sampling, nucleus sampling, and temperature scaling can be used to control the diversity and creativity of the generated text.

The fine-tuning process for ChatGPT requires careful attention to data preparation, model selection, hyperparameter tuning, and evaluation.

However, with the right approach and a well-chosen task-specific dataset, ChatGPT can be fine-tuned to generate high-quality and natural-sounding text for a wide range of applications.

Preparing The Data For Fine-Tuning

Here are some details on preparing the data for fine-tuning a ChatGPT model:

Data Collection:

The first step in preparing the data is to collect the relevant text data for the specific task. This may involve scraping websites, downloading public datasets, or collecting data from proprietary sources. It is important to ensure that the collected data is relevant to the task and that it represents the language and style of text that the ChatGPT model will be fine-tuned on.

Data Cleaning:

The next step is to clean the collected data to remove any irrelevant or low-quality content. This may involve removing duplicates, correcting misspellings, removing special characters or formatting, and removing irrelevant information such as headers, footers, or advertisements. It is important to maintain the original structure and context of the text while removing any extraneous information.

Data Preprocessing:

Once the data has been cleaned, it needs to be preprocessed to prepare it for fine-tuning. This typically involves tokenizing the text into individual words or subwords, converting the text into a numerical format that can be fed into the ChatGPT model, and splitting the data into training, validation, and test sets. Preprocessing may also involve additional steps such as lowercasing, stemming, or removing stop words, depending on the specific task and dataset.

Data Augmentation:

Data augmentation techniques can be used to increase the size and diversity of the dataset, which can improve the performance of the fine-tuned ChatGPT model. Some common data augmentation techniques include paraphrasing, back-translation, and data synthesis using generative models. These techniques can be especially useful for tasks such as language translation or text summarization, where the available data may be limited or biased.

Data Balancing:
If the dataset is imbalanced, meaning that certain classes or categories have more or less data than others, it may be necessary to balance the data to ensure that the model is not biased towards the majority class. This can be done through techniques such as oversampling, undersampling, or data weighting, which adjust the distribution of the data to create a more balanced training set.

Preparing the data for fine-tuning a ChatGPT model can be a time-consuming and challenging process, but it is crucial for achieving good performance on the target task.

By carefully selecting, cleaning, preprocessing, augmenting, and balancing the data, it is possible to fine-tune a ChatGPT model that can generate high-quality and natural-sounding text for a wide range of applications.

Here are some additional details on preparing the data for fine-tuning a ChatGPT model, along with some examples:

Data Collection:
The process of data collection can vary depending on the specific task and dataset. For example, if the task is sentiment analysis, the dataset may be collected by scraping social media sites like Twitter or Facebook for relevant tweets or posts.

If the task is language translation, the dataset may be obtained by downloading publicly available parallel corpora of text in the source and target languages.

For example, the WMT dataset is a commonly used dataset for machine translation that contains parallel corpora in multiple languages.

Data Cleaning:

Data cleaning involves removing any irrelevant or low-quality content from the collected dataset. For example, if the dataset contains duplicates, they can be removed using tools like Dedupe.

If the dataset contains misspellings, they can be corrected using spell checkers like PySpellChecker. Special characters or formatting can be removed using regular expressions or other text manipulation tools.

Here's an example of cleaning a sentence:

Original sentence: "It's raining, but I'm happy anyways!! :)"

Cleaned sentence: "It's raining, but I'm happy anyways"

Data Preprocessing:

Once the data has been cleaned, it needs to be preprocessed to prepare it for fine-tuning. This typically involves tokenizing the text into individual words or subwords, converting the text into a numerical format that can be fed into the ChatGPT model, and splitting the data into training, validation, and test sets.

Here's an example of tokenizing a sentence:

Original sentence: "I went to the park yesterday."

Tokenized sentence: ["I", "went", "to", "the", "park", "yesterday", "."]

Data Augmentation:

Data augmentation techniques can be used to increase the size and diversity of the dataset. For example, paraphrasing can be used to create new sentences with the same meaning as the original sentence, but with different wording.

Back-translation can be used to translate the dataset into a different language and then translate it back to the original language, which can introduce new variations in the text.

Here's an example of paraphrasing a sentence:

Original sentence: "The cat sat on the mat."

Paraphrased sentence: "The feline rested on the rug."

Data Balancing:

If the dataset is imbalanced, it may be necessary to balance the data to ensure that the model is not biased towards the majority class. For example, if the dataset contains 80% positive sentiment and 20% negative sentiment, undersampling can be used to remove some of the positive sentiment examples and create a more balanced dataset.

Here's an example of undersampling a dataset:

Original dataset: 100 positive sentiment examples, 25 negative sentiment examples

Undersampled dataset: 25 positive sentiment examples, 25 negative sentiment examples

These techniques can be used to prepare the data for fine-tuning a ChatGPT model and improve its performance on the target task.

By carefully selecting, cleaning, preprocessing, augmenting, and balancing the data, it is possible to fine-tune a ChatGPT model that can generate high-quality and natural-sounding text for a wide range of applications.

Choosing And Adapting
The Pre-Trained Models

In Chapter 3, we discuss the process of choosing and adapting pre-trained models for fine-tuning ChatGPT for text generation.

Pre-trained models have already been trained on a large amount of text data and can be fine-tuned for specific tasks like text generation. The pre-trained models can be obtained from various sources like Hugging Face, Google AI, or OpenAI.

The choice of pre-trained model depends on the specific task and the size of the dataset available for fine-tuning. Generally, the larger the pre-trained model, the better it performs on complex tasks.

However, larger models also require more computational resources and time for fine-tuning.

Once the appropriate pre-trained model is selected, it needs to be adapted to the specific task at hand. This involves changing the architecture and hyperparameters of the model. For example, the number of layers, hidden units, and attention heads can be modified to suit the specific task.

Let's consider an example of fine-tuning a pre-trained model for a customer service chatbot. The pre-trained model may have been trained on a large corpus of news articles and may not perform well for the chatbot task. In this case, the pre-trained model can be fine-tuned on a dataset of customer service conversations.

The model can be adapted by adding more layers and attention heads to capture the conversational context better.

The process of choosing and adapting pre-trained models is crucial for fine-tuning ChatGPT for text generation. It requires careful consideration of the specific task and the available resources for fine-tuning.

Let's dive deeper into the process of choosing and adapting pre-trained models with some examples.

Example 1: Fine-tuning for sentiment analysis
Suppose we want to fine-tune a pre-trained GPT-2 model for sentiment analysis. We can obtain a pre-trained model from Hugging Face or OpenAI and fine-tune it on a dataset of movie reviews labeled with positive or negative sentiment.

To adapt the pre-trained model, we can modify the last layer of the model to output a binary classification of positive or negative sentiment. We can also adjust the learning rate, batch size, and number of epochs to optimize the fine-tuning process.

Example 2: Fine-tuning for question answering
Suppose we want to fine-tune a pre-trained GPT-3 model for question answering. We can obtain a pre-trained model from OpenAI and fine-tune it on a dataset of questions and answers in a specific domain like healthcare or finance.

To adapt the pre-trained model, we can modify the architecture to include a question encoder and an answer decoder. We can also fine-tune the model with a larger batch size and longer sequence length to better capture the context of the questions and answers.

Example 3: Fine-tuning for chatbot
Suppose we want to fine-tune a pre-trained GPT-2 model for a customer service chatbot. We can obtain a pre-trained model from Hugging Face or OpenAI and fine-tune it on a dataset of customer service conversations. To adapt the pre-trained model, we can modify the architecture to include a conversation history encoder and a response decoder. We can also fine-tune the model with a smaller learning rate and a larger number of training epochs to capture the nuances of customer service conversations.

The process of choosing and adapting pre-trained models requires careful consideration of the specific task and the available resources for fine-tuning.

It is essential to optimize the model architecture and hyperparameters to achieve the best performance for the target task.

Here are a few more examples of choosing and adapting pre-trained models:

Example 4: Fine-tuning for machine translation
Suppose we want to build a machine translation system from English to French. We can obtain a pre-trained GPT-2 model from Hugging Face or OpenAI and fine-tune it on a dataset of parallel English-French sentences.

To adapt the pre-trained model, we can modify the architecture to include an encoder for English sentences and a decoder for French sentences. We can also adjust the learning rate, batch size, and number of epochs to optimize the fine-tuning process.

Example 5: Fine-tuning for named entity recognition
Suppose we want to build a named entity recognition system for detecting entities like people, organizations, and locations in text. We can obtain a pre-trained BERT model from Hugging Face or Google and fine-tune it on a dataset of labeled entities in text. To adapt the pre-trained model, we can modify the architecture to include a classifier for each entity type.

We can also fine-tune the model with a smaller learning rate and a larger number of training epochs to capture the subtle variations in entity recognition.

In general, the process of fine-tuning pre-trained models involves selecting the right model architecture, optimizing the hyperparameters, and fine-tuning the model on a relevant dataset.

With careful planning and experimentation, we can achieve state-of-the-art performance for a wide range of natural language processing tasks.

CHAPTER 4
TEXT GENERATION TECHNIQUES AND EVALUATION

In Chapter 4, we will explore various text generation techniques and evaluation methods for ChatGPT models.

Here's some of what we'll cover:

Autoregressive Text Generation

We'll start by discussing the autoregressive text generation method, which is the most common approach used by ChatGPT models. We'll explain how the model generates text one word at a time, based on the previous words in the sequence.

We'll also discuss different sampling methods, such as greedy decoding and beam search, and how they affect the quality and diversity of generated text.

Non-Autoregressive Text Generation

Next, we'll explore non-autoregressive text generation techniques, which aim to generate text in parallel instead of sequentially. We'll explain how these models differ from autoregressive models, and discuss the challenges and opportunities of non-autoregressive text generation.

Text Evaluation Metrics

After covering text generation techniques, we'll move on to discussing text evaluation metrics.

We'll explain the common evaluation metrics used for generated text, such as perplexity, BLEU score, and human evaluation.

We'll also discuss the limitations and shortcomings of these metrics, and how to choose the most appropriate evaluation method for a given task.

Bias and Fairness in Text Generation

We'll address the important issue of bias and fairness in text generation. We'll explain how biases can be introduced into generated text, and the impact of these biases on downstream applications.

We'll also discuss methods for detecting and mitigating bias in text generation, and the ethical implications of deploying biased models in real-world scenarios.

By the end of Chapter 4, students will have a comprehensive understanding of various text generation techniques and evaluation methods for ChatGPT models, as well as the ethical considerations involved in generating text with these models.

Generating Text with Various Techniques such as Beam Search and Nucleus Sampling

Generating text is a fascinating area of Natural Language Processing (NLP) that involves creating coherent and meaningful sentences or paragraphs based on a given context or topic. In recent years, the advancements in deep learning techniques have led to significant improvements in the quality of generated text. This chapter will focus on two popular techniques for generating text, Beam Search and Nucleus Sampling.

Beam Search

Beam search is a simple but effective algorithm for generating text. It works by maintaining a fixed number of candidate sequences, called beams, at each step of the generation process. The number of beams is a hyperparameter that can be set based on the complexity of the problem and the available computational resources.

At each step, the algorithm generates the top-k most probable next words for each beam and then creates k new beams by appending each of the k words to each of the k previous beams. The k beams with the highest probability are retained, and the process continues until a termination condition is met.

Beam search can be further improved by incorporating a length normalization factor that penalizes longer sequences. This is because longer sequences tend to have lower probabilities due to the nature of language. By using a length normalization factor, the algorithm can generate more coherent and concise text.

Nucleus Sampling

Nucleus sampling, also known as top-p sampling, is a probabilistic algorithm for generating text. It works by first computing the probability distribution over the vocabulary of possible next words given the current context. The algorithm then selects the smallest set of words that account for a certain percentage p of the total probability mass. This set of words is called the nucleus. The algorithm then samples a word from the nucleus with a probability proportional to its original probability.

Nucleus sampling has several advantages over other sampling techniques, such as pure random sampling. First, it allows for a controlled amount of randomness, which can produce more diverse and interesting text.

Second, it is less likely to produce nonsensical or irrelevant text, as it only considers words that are most likely to occur in a given context. Finally, it can be used to generate text with different levels of creativity by varying the value of p.

Comparison

Both Beam search and Nucleus sampling are effective techniques for generating text. Beam search is a deterministic algorithm that always produces the same output given the same input, making it ideal for tasks that require consistency and reproducibility. It is also computationally efficient, as it only considers a fixed number of candidate sequences at each step.

On the other hand, Nucleus sampling is a probabilistic algorithm that introduces randomness and diversity into the generation process. It is more flexible than Beam search, as it allows for different levels of creativity and can produce more varied and interesting text. However, it can be more computationally expensive than Beam search, as it requires computing the probability distribution over the entire vocabulary at each step.

Beam search and Nucleus sampling are two popular techniques for generating text. They have different strengths and weaknesses and can be used for different types of tasks.

Practitioners should consider the characteristics of their problem and the available computational resources before choosing which technique to use. In general, Beam search is a good choice for tasks that require consistency and efficiency, while Nucleus sampling is better suited for tasks that require creativity and diversity.

Let's dive a bit deeper into both techniques and provide some concrete examples.

Beam Search

Beam search is a widely used technique for text generation, especially in tasks such as machine translation and language modeling.

One of the main advantages of beam search is that it allows for fast and efficient generation of text, making it suitable for real-time applications.

Let's take the example of machine translation, where the goal is to translate a sentence from one language to another. Suppose we want to translate the sentence **"Je Suis Un Chat"** from French to English.

Using a pre-trained neural machine translation model, we can generate a list of candidate translations for each word in the input sentence.

The list of candidate translations for the first word "Je" might look like this:

```
Beam size: 3
1. I
2. My
3. Me
```

We can then use beam search to select the most probable translation sequence given the input sentence and the pre-trained model.

Suppose we set the beam size to 2, and we want to generate the top 2 most probable translations for the entire sentence.

The beam search process might look like this:

Step 1:
>   Beam 1: [I]
>   Beam 2: [My]

Step 2:
>   Beam 1: [I, am]
>   Beam 2: [My, am]

Step 3:
>   Beam 1: [I, am, a]
>   Beam 2: [My, am, a]

Step 4:
>   Beam 1: [I, am, a, cat]
>   Beam 2: [My, am, a, cat]

Output:
>   "I am a cat"

In this example, the beam search algorithm selected the sequence with the highest probability as the output sequence.

Beam search allowed us to generate the translation quickly and efficiently while maintaining the coherence and consistency of the output.

Nucleus Sampling

Nucleus sampling is a relatively new technique for text generation that has gained popularity in recent years. It is particularly useful in tasks where we want to generate diverse and creative text while maintaining the coherence and relevance of the output.

Let's take the example of generating a product review based on a given product description. Suppose we have a pre-trained language model that can generate product reviews based on the input product description. We can use nucleus sampling to generate reviews that are both creative and relevant to the product description.

Suppose we want to generate a product review for a smartphone with the following description:

> "The smartphone has a large screen, a powerful processor, and a long battery life."

Using nucleus sampling, we can first generate a list of candidate words based on the input description. The list might look like this:

Nucleus size: 0.8
1. Screen
2. Processor
3. Battery
4. Device
5. Performance
6. Display
7. Longevity
8. Life

We can then sample a review from the nucleus by selecting a set of words that account for 80% of the total probability mass. Suppose we sample the following words:

"The device has a long battery life and impressive performance."

This review is both creative and relevant to the input description, as it highlights the key features of the smartphone while also being unique and interesting.

Comparison

In terms of their strengths and weaknesses, beam search is generally more deterministic and efficient, while nucleus sampling is more flexible and creative. Beam search can produce consistent and coherent output, but it may lack creativity.

Evaluating the Quality of Generated Text Using Metrics like Perplexity and BLEU Score

Evaluating the quality of generated text is an important task in natural language generation. There are several metrics that can be used to assess the quality of generated text, including perplexity and BLEU score.

Perplexity

Perplexity is a widely used metric for evaluating the quality of language models. It measures how well a language model predicts a sequence of tokens. The lower the perplexity, the better the language model.

Perplexity is calculated as the inverse probability of the test set, normalized by the number of words in the test set.

Mathematically, perplexity is defined as:

$$\text{perplexity} = \exp(-\,\text{sum}(\log P(w\_i)) / N)$$

where $P(w\_i)$ is the probability of the i-th word in the test set, N is the total number of words in the test set, and the sum is taken over all words in the test set.

To calculate perplexity for generated text, we can use the same formula by treating the generated text as the test set and the language model as the probability distribution.

Bleu Score

BLEU (Bilingual Evaluation Understudy) score is a widely used metric for evaluating the quality of machine translation systems. It measures the similarity between a generated translation and one or more reference translations.

BLEU score ranges from 0 to 1, with higher scores indicating better translation quality. The score is calculated by comparing the generated translation to one or more reference translations and calculating the n-gram overlap between them.

The basic formula for calculating the BLEU score is:

```r
rCopy code
BLEU = BP * exp(sum(log(p_n)) / n)
```

where BP is the brevity penalty, which penalizes translations that are shorter than the reference translations. The term p_n is the precision of n-grams, which measures the overlap between the generated translation and the reference translations.

To calculate the BLEU score for generated text, we need to have one or more reference translations.

For example, if we are generating product reviews, we can use existing reviews as the reference translations and calculate the BLEU score of the generated reviews against them.

Comparison

Perplexity and BLEU score are both useful metrics for evaluating the quality of generated text, but they have different strengths and weaknesses.

Perplexity is a more general metric that can be used for any type of text generation, while BLEU score is more specific to machine translation. Perplexity is also more sensitive to the fluency and grammaticality of the generated text, while BLEU score is more sensitive to the accuracy and relevance of the generated text.

Ultimately, the choice of metric depends on the specific task and goals of the text generation system.

Here are some examples of using perplexity and BLEU score to evaluate the quality of generated text:

Example 1: Language Modeling

Suppose we have a language model trained on a corpus of news articles and we want to evaluate the quality of its generated text. We can use perplexity to measure how well the language model predicts the test set of news articles. For example, we can split the corpus into a training set and a test set, and calculate the perplexity of the language model on the test set. A lower perplexity indicates better language modeling performance.

Example 2: Machine Translation

Suppose we have a machine translation system that translates English sentences to French. We want to evaluate the quality of its translations using BLEU score. We can use a dataset of English sentences and their corresponding French translations as the reference translations. For example, we can split the dataset into a training set and a test set, and calculate the BLEU score of the machine translation system on the test set. A higher BLEU score indicates better translation quality.

In practice, evaluating the quality of generated text is often more complex than these simple examples, as there are many factors that can affect the quality of the generated text, such as the diversity, coherence, and creativity of the generated text.

Therefore, it's important to carefully choose the appropriate evaluation metrics and datasets that best capture the quality of the generated text for the specific task and application.

CHAPTER 5
A.I. N.L.P. PROMPT PRACTITIONER APPLICATIONS

In Chapter 5 of the A.I. N.L.P. Prompt Practitioner textbook, we will explore several applications of A.I. N.L.P. Prompting, including:

Chatbots: One of the most popular applications of A.I. N.L.P. Prompting is chatbots. Chatbots are conversational agents that can interact with users in natural language.

With A.I. N.L.P. Prompting, we can train chatbots to provide customer support, answer questions, and engage in casual conversation with users.

We will learn how to train chatbots using various techniques such as fine-tuning and transfer learning, and how to evaluate their performance using metrics such as perplexity and human evaluation.

Text Generation

A.I. N.L.P. Prompting can also be used for text generation, such as generating product descriptions, news articles, and poetry. We will learn how to train language models using various techniques such as masked language modeling and causal language modeling, and how to generate text using techniques such as beam search and nucleus sampling.

We will also learn how to evaluate the quality of generated text using metrics such as perplexity and BLEU score.

Text Classification

A.I. N.L.P. Prompting can be used for text classification tasks, such as sentiment analysis, topic classification, and spam detection. We will learn how to fine-tune pre-trained language models for text classification tasks, and how to evaluate their performance using metrics such as accuracy, precision, recall, and F1 score.

Question Answering
A.I. N.L.P. Prompting can also be used for question answering tasks, such as answering trivia questions or providing technical support. We will learn how to train question answering models using techniques such as fine-tuning and extractive question answering, and how to evaluate their performance using metrics such as F1 score and accuracy.

By the end of the chapter, students will have a solid understanding of how to apply A.I. N.L.P. Prompting in various text-based applications and how to evaluate the performance of their models.

Here are some more details and examples of the applications of A.I. N.L.P. Prompt:

Chatbots:
Chatbots have become increasingly popular in recent years, as they can provide quick and efficient customer support and engage in natural language conversations with users. A.I. N.L.P. Prompting can be used to train chatbots that can understand and respond to users' requests in a personalized and natural way. For example, a customer service chatbot for an e-commerce website can help users navigate the website, provide information about products, and answer questions about shipping and returns.

Text Generation:
Text generation is another important application of A.I. N.L.P. Prompt. Language models trained with A.I. N.L.P. Prompting can generate high-quality text that is coherent and relevant to the given prompt. For example, a language model trained on a corpus of movie scripts can generate new movie dialogue that sounds like it was written by a professional screenwriter.

Text Classification:
Text classification is a common task in natural language processing that involves categorizing text into predefined categories such as sentiment, topic, or spam. A.I. N.L.P. Prompting can be used to fine-tune pre-trained language models for text classification tasks. For example, a language model pre-trained on a large corpus of text can be fine-tuned on a smaller dataset of movie reviews to perform sentiment analysis.

Question Answering:
Question answering is a task that involves answering natural language questions based on a given context. A.I. N.L.P. Prompting can be used to train models for question answering tasks, such as answering trivia questions or providing technical support.

For example, a language model trained on a large corpus of Wikipedia articles can be used to answer general knowledge questions.

The applications of A.I. N.L.P. Prompting are diverse and can be applied in a variety of domains, from customer service to creative writing.

As with any machine learning model, it's important to carefully evaluate the performance of A.I. N.L.P. Prompting models on real-world datasets and consider ethical and interpretability concerns.

Practical Applications of A.I. N.L.P. Prompting Practitioner such as ChatBots Language Translation, and Content Creation

Here are some practical applications for A.I. N.L.P. Prompting Practitioner:

Chatbots

As mentioned earlier, chatbots are one of the most popular applications of A.I. N.L.P. Prompt. Chatbots can be used in various domains, such as customer service, marketing, and personal assistants.

With A.I. N.L.P. Prompt, chatbots can be trained to understand and respond to natural language queries, personalize responses, and provide recommendations. For example, a chatbot for an e-commerce website can help users navigate the website, provide product recommendations, and answer questions about shipping and returns.

Language Translation

A.I. N.L.P. Prompting can be used for language translation tasks, such as translating text from one language to another. With the help of pre-trained language models, A.I. N.L.P. Prompting can generate high-quality translations that preserve the meaning of the source text.

For example, a language model trained on a large corpus of English text can be fine-tuned for French-to-English translation.

Content Creation

A.I. N.L.P. Prompting can be used for content creation tasks, such as generating product descriptions, news articles, and social media posts. With A.I. N.L.P. Prompt, language models can generate high-quality text that is coherent and relevant to the given prompt.

For example, a language model trained on a corpus of blog posts can generate new blog posts that sound like they were written by a professional blogger.

Question Answering

A.I. N.L.P. Prompting can be used for question answering tasks, such as answering trivia questions or providing technical support. With the help of pre-trained language models, A.I. N.L.P. Prompting can understand the context of the question and generate accurate answers.

For example, a language model trained on a large corpus of Wikipedia articles can be fine-tuned for general knowledge question answering.

Personalized Marketing:

A.I. N.L.P. Prompting can be used to create personalized marketing messages for individual customers. With the help of pre-trained language models, A.I. N.L.P. Prompting can generate marketing messages that are tailored to each customer's interests and preferences.

Sentiment Analysis:

A.I. N.L.P. Prompting can be used to perform sentiment analysis, which involves determining the sentiment (positive, negative, or neutral) of a piece of text.

With the help of pre-trained language models, A.I. N.L.P. Prompting can accurately classify the sentiment of text, which can be useful in various domains, such as market research and social media monitoring.

Summarization:

A.I. N.L.P. Prompting can be used for text summarization tasks, which involve generating a summary of a longer piece of text. With the help of pre-trained language models, A.I. N.L.P. Prompting can generate summaries that capture the main points of the text.

Speech Recognition:

A.I. N.L.P. Prompting can be used for speech recognition tasks, which involve transcribing spoken language into text.

With the help of pre-trained language models, A.I. N.L.P. Prompting can accurately transcribe spoken language, which can be useful in various domains, such as call center analytics and voice assistants.

Language Modeling:
A.I. N.L.P. Prompting can be used for language modeling tasks, which involve predicting the next word in a sequence of words. With the help of pre-trained language models, A.I. N.L.P. Prompting can generate high-quality text that follows the patterns and structures of natural language.

Image Captioning:
A.I. N.L.P. Prompting can be used for image captioning tasks, which involve generating a caption that describes the content of an image. With the help of pre-trained language models and computer vision models, A.I. N.L.P. Prompting can generate accurate and descriptive captions for images.

Text Completion:
A.I. N.L.P. Prompting can be used for text completion tasks, which involve predicting the next word or sequence of words in a sentence. With the help of pre-trained language models, A.I. N.L.P. Prompting can generate text that completes a given prompt.

Paraphrasing:
A.I. N.L.P. Prompting can be used for paraphrasing tasks, which involve restating a sentence or passage in different words while preserving the meaning. With the help of pre-trained language models, A.I. N.L.P. Prompting can generate paraphrases that are grammatically correct and semantically accurate.

Content Moderation:
A.I. N.L.P. Prompting can be used for content moderation tasks, which involve detecting and removing inappropriate or harmful content. With the help of pre-trained language models, A.I. N.L.P. Prompting can identify hate speech, bullying, and other types of harmful content.

Recommendation Systems:
A.I. N.L.P. Prompting can be used for recommendation systems, which involve recommending products, services, or content to users based on their preferences and behavior.

With the help of pre-trained language models, A.I. N.L.P. Prompting can generate personalized recommendations that are tailored to each user's interests and needs.

Knowledge Graph Completion:

A.I. N.L.P. Prompting can be used for knowledge graph completion, which involves predicting missing relationships between entities in a knowledge graph. With the help of pre-trained language models, A.I. N.L.P. Prompting can generate accurate predictions for missing relationships.

Customer Service Chatbots:

A.I. N.L.P. Prompting can be used to create customer service chatbots that can handle customer queries and complaints. With the help of pre-trained language models, A.I. N.L.P. Prompting can generate human-like responses to customer queries and provide a personalized customer experience.

Text Generation for Games:

A.I. N.L.P. Prompting can be used to generate text for games such as RPGs (role-playing games) and interactive fiction. With the help of pre-trained language models, A.I. N.L.P. Prompting can generate dynamic and engaging narratives that respond to user actions.

Question Answering:

A.I. N.L.P. Prompting can be used for question answering tasks, which involve answering questions posed in natural language. With the help of pre-trained language models, A.I. N.L.P. Prompting can generate accurate and relevant answers to a wide range of questions.

Language Translation:

A.I. N.L.P. Prompting can be used for language translation tasks, which involve translating text from one language to another.

With the help of pre-trained language models, A.I. N.L.P. Prompting can generate high-quality translations that preserve the meaning and nuance of the original text.

Text Classification:

A.I. N.L.P. Prompting can be used for text classification tasks, which involve classifying text into predefined categories. With the help of pre-trained language models, A.I. N.L.P. Prompting can accurately classify text into categories such as spam, sentiment, and topic.

Content Generation for Social Media:
A.I. N.L.P. Prompting can be used to generate content for social media platforms such as Twitter and Instagram.

With the help of pre-trained language models, A.I. N.L.P. Prompting can generate engaging and shareable content that is tailored to each platform and audience.

Text-to-Speech: A.I. N.L.P.
Prompting can be used for text-to-speech tasks, which involve converting written text into spoken language. With the help of pre-trained language models, A.I. N.L.P. Prompting can generate natural-sounding speech that is indistinguishable from human speech.

Medical Diagnosis:
A.I. N.L.P. Prompting can be used for medical diagnosis tasks, which involve analyzing patient symptoms and generating a diagnosis.

With the help of pre-trained language models, A.I. N.L.P. Prompting can generate accurate diagnoses based on a patient's symptoms and medical history.

ChatOps:
A.I. N.L.P. Prompting can be used for ChatOps, which is a method of communication between developers and IT teams that involves using chatbots to automate tasks and workflows.

With the help of pre-trained language models, A.I. N.L.P. Prompting can automate tasks such as deploying code and troubleshooting issues.

These are just a few examples of the practical applications of A.I. N.L.P. Prompt. As A.I. N.L.P. Prompting continues to improve, we can expect to see it being used in a variety of other domains, such as healthcare, finance, and education.

Tips for Building Effective Applications as an A.I. NLP Prompt Practitioner

Here are some tips for building effective applications with A.I. N.L.P. Prompting Practitioner:

Define the Problem:
Clearly define the problem you are trying to solve with your application. This will help you choose the appropriate architecture, models, and data sources to build your application.

Choose the Right Model:
Choose the right pre-trained language model for your application based on the task you are trying to perform. There are various pre-trained models available, each optimized for different tasks such as language generation, language translation, text classification, and question answering.

Fine-Tune the Model:
Fine-tune the pre-trained model on your specific dataset to improve its performance on your task. This will help the model learn the specific nuances and characteristics of your data.

Data Preprocessing:
Preprocess your data to ensure that it is clean and consistent. This includes removing duplicate entries, handling missing values, and standardizing the format of the data.

Input Formatting:
Format the input data to match the format expected by the pre-trained model. This includes tokenizing the input text, handling special characters, and padding the input sequences.

Evaluation Metrics: Choose appropriate evaluation metrics for your application. This will help you measure the performance of your model and identify areas for improvement. Common evaluation metrics include perplexity, BLEU score, and accuracy.

Error Analysis: Perform error analysis to identify common errors made by the model and the underlying causes. This will help you improve the model's performance and identify areas for future research.

Test Your Application: Test your application thoroughly to ensure that it works as expected and can handle a wide range of inputs and scenarios. This includes testing for edge cases, handling unexpected inputs, and validating the output.

Monitor Performance: Monitor the performance of your application in production to identify any issues or errors that arise. This will help you maintain the performance and reliability of your application over time.

Continual Improvement: Continually improve your application over time by incorporating feedback from users and monitoring the latest research in the field. This will help you stay up to date with the latest developments and ensure that your application remains effective and relevant.

Consider User Experience: Consider the user experience when designing and developing your application. This includes factors such as usability, ease of use, and accessibility.

Choose the Right Hardware: Choose the right hardware for your application, including GPUs, CPUs, and memory. This will help you achieve optimal performance and scalability.

Optimize for Speed:

Optimize your application for speed by using techniques such as caching, batch processing, and parallelization. This will help you achieve faster response times and reduce latency.

Handle Out-of-Vocabulary Words:

Handle out-of-vocabulary words by using techniques such as subword tokenization, word embeddings, and character-level models. This will help you handle rare or uncommon words that may not be present in the pre-trained model's vocabulary.

Handle Multi-lingual Data:

Handle multi-lingual data by using techniques such as language identification, translation, and transliteration. This will help you handle data in different languages and improve the accuracy of your application.

Incorporate Human Feedback:

Incorporate human feedback into your application by using techniques such as active learning, human-in-the-loop, and crowdsourcing. This will help you improve the accuracy and relevance of your application over time.

Security and Privacy:

Consider security and privacy when developing your application. This includes securing data in transit and at rest, implementing access controls, and ensuring compliance with relevant regulations such as GDPR and CCPA.

Avoid Bias:

Avoid bias in your application by using diverse and representative datasets, testing for bias, and incorporating fairness and ethical considerations into your development process.

Documentation and Testing:
Ensure that your application is well-documented and thoroughly tested. This includes documenting the input and output formats, providing clear instructions for users, and testing for edge cases and error handling.

Collaboration and Community:
Collaborate with other developers and researchers in the field, and participate in the broader community to share knowledge and best practices, and stay up to date with the latest developments in the field.

CHAPTER 6
A.I. NLP PROMPT PRACTITIONER
BEST PRACTICES

Chapter 6 of the A.I. NLP Prompt Practitioner textbook covers best practices for working with the A.I. NLP Prompt framework. Here are some of the key topics that are covered in this chapter

Data Preprocessing

Data preprocessing is a crucial step in working with any machine learning framework, and A.I. NLP Prompt is no exception. The chapter covers best practices for cleaning and formatting data to ensure that it is ready to be used with the framework.

Hyperparameter Tuning

Hyperparameter tuning is the process of optimizing the parameters of your model to achieve the best possible performance. The chapter covers best practices for selecting and tuning hyperparameters such as learning rate, batch size, and number of epochs.

Model Training

Model training is the process of training your A.I. NLP Prompt model on your data. The chapter covers best practices for model training, including techniques such as early stopping, learning rate scheduling, and gradient clipping.

Model Evaluation

Model evaluation is the process of testing your model's performance on a separate test set. The chapter covers best practices for model evaluation, including metrics such as perplexity, BLEU score, and human evaluation.

Deployment

Deployment is the process of making your A.I. NLP Prompt application available to users. The chapter covers best practices for deploying your application, including techniques such as containerization, serverless architecture, and API design.

Monitoring and Maintenance

Monitoring and maintenance are crucial for ensuring the long-term success of your A.I. NLP Prompt application. The chapter covers best practices for monitoring your application's performance, handling errors and exceptions, and ensuring that it stays up to date with the latest developments in the field.

Ethics and Fairness

Ethics and fairness are increasingly important considerations in the development of machine learning applications. The chapter covers best practices for ensuring that your A.I. NLP Prompt application is fair and ethical, including techniques such as bias testing, interpretability, and transparency.

Data Preprocessing

To preprocess your data for A.I. NLP Prompt, you should start by cleaning and formatting it. This might involve removing punctuation and other non-text characters, normalizing capitalization and spacing, and splitting your data into training, validation, and test sets. For example, if you are building a chatbot, you might preprocess your data by cleaning up chat logs and dividing them into separate training and test sets.

Hyperparameter Tuning

Hyperparameter tuning is an iterative process that involves testing different combinations of hyperparameters to find the best set of values for your model. To do this effectively, you should start with a reasonable set of default values and then experiment with different values for each hyperparameter. For example, if you are building a language model, you might experiment with different values for the learning rate, batch size, and number of epochs.

Model Training

Model training involves using your preprocessed data to train your A.I. NLP Prompt model. To do this effectively, you should use techniques such as early stopping, learning rate scheduling, and gradient clipping. For example, you might use early stopping to automatically stop training when the model's performance on the validation set stops improving.

Model Evaluation

Model evaluation involves testing your model's performance on a separate test set. To do this effectively, you should use metrics such as perplexity, BLEU score, and human evaluation. For example, if you are building a language model, you might use perplexity to measure how well the model can predict the next word in a sequence of text.

Deployment

Deployment involves making your A.I. NLP Prompt application available to users. To do this effectively, you should consider using techniques such as containerization, serverless architecture, and API design. For example, if you are building a chatbot, you might use a serverless architecture to deploy your application to the cloud, and an API design to allow users to interact with your chatbot through a web interface.

Monitoring And Maintenance

Monitoring and maintenance involves keeping your A.I. NLP Prompt application running smoothly over time. To do this effectively, you should use techniques such as logging, error handling, and version control. For example, you might use logging to track how users are interacting with your chatbot, and version control to keep track of changes to your application over time.

Ethics And Fairness

Ethics and fairness are important considerations in the development of any machine learning application. To ensure that your A.I. NLP Prompt application is fair and ethical, you should consider using techniques such as bias testing, interpretability, and transparency. For example, you might use bias testing to identify and mitigate any biases in your chatbot's responses, and interpretability to help users understand how the chatbot is making its decisions.

Chapter 6 provides a comprehensive guide to best practices for working with A.I. NLP Prompt, covering everything from data preprocessing to deployment and maintenance. By following these best practices, developers can ensure that their A.I. NLP Prompt applications are accurate, scalable, and ethical.

Best Practices for Generating High-Quality Text

Here are some best practices for generating high-quality text with A.I. NLP Prompt

Use high-quality data
The quality of your text generation is directly related to the quality of your data. Use clean, relevant, and diverse data to train your model.

Fine-tune the model
Fine-tuning a pre-trained model on your specific task can improve text generation quality. Use the right hyperparameters, and experiment with different architectures and pre-trained models.

Use a large enough training dataset
The more data you have, the better your model will perform. Use a large enough training dataset to ensure that your model has enough data to learn from.

Use diverse and relevant prompts
Use diverse and relevant prompts to generate text that is specific to your use case. Consider the context in which the text will be generated and use prompts that are appropriate.

Use appropriate length of generated text
Generate text of appropriate length based on the requirements of your use case. Longer text may contain more errors, and shorter text may not provide enough information.

Use appropriate decoding techniques
Use decoding techniques such as beam search and nucleus sampling to generate high-quality text. Experiment with different parameters to find the best decoding technique for your use case.

Monitor Generated Text Quality

Monitor the quality of the generated text using metrics such as perplexity, BLEU score, and human evaluation. Use these metrics to improve the quality of your text generation.

Post-Process The Generated Text

Post-process the generated text to correct errors and improve readability. Use techniques such as language model correction and text normalization to improve the quality of the generated text.

Use The Right Generation Task

Choose the right generation task for your use case. Text generation can be used for a variety of tasks, such as summarization, translation, and content creation.

Evaluate Ethical Implications

Evaluate the ethical implications of the generated text. Consider the im
pact of the text on different communities and take steps to mitigate any negative effects.

Use Domain-Specific Data

Use domain-specific data to train your model if you're working on a task that requires domain-specific language. For example, if you're building a chatbot for a financial institution, use financial data to train your model.

Use Data Augmentation Techniques

Use data augmentation techniques such as synonym replacement, word swapping, and random deletion to increase the diversity of your training data.

Regularly Update Your Model
Regularly update your model with new data to ensure that it stays up-to-date and continues to generate high-quality text.

Use Ensembling
Use ensembling techniques such as bagging and boosting to combine the output of multiple models for improved text generation.

Consider Pre-Processing Techniques
Use pre-processing techniques such as text normalization and tokenization to improve the quality of your training data.

Use Attention Mechanisms
Use attention mechanisms to improve the performance of your model on long sequences of text. Attention mechanisms allow the model to focus on the most relevant parts of the input sequence.

Monitor The Training Process
Monitor the training process to ensure that the model is converging and not overfitting or underfitting the data.

Use Transfer Learning
Use transfer learning techniques to leverage pre-trained models for your specific use case. For example, fine-tune a pre-trained language model on your task-specific data.

Use Human Feedback
 Incorporate human feedback into the text generation process to improve the quality of the generated text. This can include using human annotation for training data or collecting feedback from users of the generated text.

Consider The Trade-Off Between Quality And Speed

Consider the trade-off between the quality of the generated text and the speed at which it is generated. Depending on your use case, you may need to optimize for speed or quality. For example, in a chatbot, speed may be more important than quality if the goal is to provide quick responses to users.

/ Select appropriate hyperparameters such as learning rate, batch size, and number of epochs to optimize the performance of your model. Tuning hyperparameters can significantly improve the quality of generated text.

Use A Diverse Set Of Prompts

Use a diverse set of prompts during training to encourage the model to generate text that covers a wide range of topics and styles.

Use A Mix Of Training Techniques

Use a mix of training techniques such as supervised learning, unsupervised learning, and reinforcement learning to improve the quality of generated text.

Use Knowledge Distillation

Use knowledge distillation techniques to transfer the knowledge of a larger pre-trained model to a smaller model that can generate high-quality text in real-time.

Use Regularization Techniques

Use regularization techniques such as dropout and weight decay to prevent overfitting and improve the generalization ability of the model.

Use Appropriate Evaluation Metrics

Select appropriate evaluation metrics such as ROUGE, METEOR, and CIDEr to evaluate the quality of generated text. Different metrics may be appropriate for different use cases.

Use Diverse Training Data Sources
Use diverse training data sources such as social media, news articles, and scientific publications to increase the variety of language styles and topics covered in the training data.

Use Semi-Supervised Learning
Use semi-supervised learning techniques to leverage a small amount of labeled data and a large amount of unlabeled data to train a high-quality text generation model.

Use Parallel Computing
Use parallel computing techniques to accelerate the training process and generate high-quality text in real-time.

Use Active Learning
Use active learning techniques to select the most informative samples for annotation and improve the quality of the training data. Active learning can help reduce the cost of human annotation and improve the overall performance of the model.

<h1 align="center">Strategies for Dealing with Common Challenges
in Text Generation</h1>

Here are some strategies for dealing with common challenges in text generation:

Avoid Repetitive Text
Use techniques like beam search, nucleus sampling, and diverse beam search to generate diverse and non-repetitive text.

Handle Rare Words And Out-Of-Vocabulary (Oov) Tokens
Use techniques like subword tokenization or byte-pair encoding (BPE) to handle rare words and OOV tokens.

Deal With The Problem Of Vanishing Gradients
Use techniques like residual connections, skip connections, or gradient clipping to avoid vanishing gradients and ensure that the model can learn from long-term dependencies.

Address The Problem Of Low Sample Efficiency
Use transfer learning techniques to fine-tune pre-trained models on your specific task. This can significantly reduce the amount of data required to train a high-quality text generation model.

Avoid Generating Off-Topic Text
Use techniques like conditional generation or topic modeling to ensure that the generated text stays on-topic and coherent.

Address The Problem Of Biased Language
Use techniques like debiasing or fairness constraints to ensure that the generated text is free of gender, racial, or other biases.

Deal With The Problem Of Generating Inconsistent Text
Use consistency constraints or consistency models to ensure that the generated text is consistent with the input context.

Handle The Problem Of Generating Inappropriate Text
Use censorship techniques or sentiment analysis to ensure that the generated text is appropriate for the intended audience and does not contain offensive or inappropriate language.

Avoid Generating Unrealistic Text
Use realism constraints or realism models to ensure that the generated text is realistic and plausible.

Address The Problem Of Generating Incomplete Text
Use techniques like sequence-to-sequence models or conditional language models to generate complete and coherent sentences or paragraphs.

Handle The Problem Of Generating Redundant Or Repetitive Text
Use techniques like repetition penalty or history pruning to reduce the generation of redundant or repetitive text.

Address The Problem Of Generating Text With Grammatical Errors
Use language models trained on large amounts of data to generate grammatically correct text, and use grammar checking tools to identify and correct errors.

Avoid Generating Text That Is Too Verbose Or Too Concise
Use techniques like length constraints or length normalization to ensure that the generated text is of an appropriate length.

Deal With The Problem Of Generating Text With Incorrect Or Inconsistent Factual Information:
Use fact-checking tools or knowledge graphs to ensure that the generated text is factually accurate and consistent.

Handle The Problem Of Generating Text That Is Difficult To Read Or Understand:
Use readability metrics or readability formulas to ensure that the generated text is easy to read and understand.

Address The Problem Of Generating Text With Insufficient Or Irrelevant Information :
Use techniques like information retrieval or knowledge extraction to ensure that the generated text contains sufficient and relevant information.

Avoid Generating Text With A Biased Tone Or Perspective:
Use techniques like sentiment analysis or tone detection to ensure that the generated text has an appropriate tone and perspective.

Deal With The Problem Of Generating Text With Unnatural Or Awkward Phrasing:
Use techniques like language model finetuning or human evaluation to ensure that the generated text is natural and fluent.

Handle The Problem Of Generating Text In Different Languages Or Dialects:
Use language-specific models or multi-lingual models to generate text in different languages or dialects.

Address The Problem Of Generating Text In Specific Domains Or Contexts :
Use domain-specific or context-specific models to generate text that is tailored to specific domains or contexts.

Address The Problem Of Generating Text With Inappropriate
Or Offensive Language :
Use profanity filters or offensive language detection to ensure
that the generated text is appropriate and respectful.

Avoid Generating Text That Is Too Generic Or
Lacks Specificity :
Use techniques like named entity recognition or topic modeling
to ensure that the generated text is specific and relevant to the
given context.

Deal With The Problem Of Generating Text With Incomplete
Or Ambiguous Information :
Use techniques like question-answering or summarization
to ensure that the generated text provides complete and
unambiguous information.

Handle The Problem Of Generating Text That Lacks
 Coherence Or Cohesion:
Use techniques like coherence modeling or discourse analysis to
ensure that the generated text is coherent and cohesive.

Address The Problem Of Generating Text With Incorrect
 Or Inappropriate Style :
Use style transfer or style adaptation techniques to ensure that
the generated text matches the desired style.

Avoid Generating Text That Is Biased Towards Certain Entities
Or Viewpoints :
Use techniques like debiasing or fairness metrics to ensure that
the generated text is fair and unbiased.

Deal With The Problem Of Generating Text That Is
Too Predictable Or Formulaic :
Use techniques like creative generation or diversity promotion
to ensure that the generated text is creative and diverse.

Handle The Problem Of Generating Text That Is Too Dependent On The Input Or Context :
Use techniques like topic conditioning or prompt engineering to ensure that the generated text is not overly dependent on the input or context.

Address The Problem Of Generating Text That Is Too Generic Or Lacks Personalization :
Use techniques like user modeling or personalization strategies to ensure that the generated text is personalized and tailored to the individual user.

Avoid Generating Text That Is Too Complex Or Technical For The Intended Audience :
Use techniques like readability analysis or simplification to ensure that the generated text is appropriate for the intended audience.

Handle The Problem Of Generating Text That Is Too Short Or Too Long :
Use techniques like length control or token control to ensure that the generated text is of appropriate length.

Avoid Generating Text That Is Too Repetitive Or Redundant :
Use techniques like diversity promotion or novelty detection to ensure that the generated text is not overly repetitive or redundant.

Address The Problem Of Generating Text That Is Too Literal Or Lacks Creativity:
Use techniques like metaphor generation or figurative language generation to ensure that the generated text is creative and imaginative.

Deal With The Problem Of Generating Text That Is
Too Formal Or Informal For The Intended Audience :
Use techniques like register adaptation or style transfer to
ensure that the generated text matches the desired level of
formality or informality.

Handle The Problem Of Generating Text That Is Too
Dependent On The Training Data Or Model Architecture:
Use techniques like data augmentation or model ensembling to
ensure that the generated text is not overly dependent on the
training data or model architecture.

Address The Problem Of Generating Text That Is
Too Subjective Or Lacks Objectivity :
Use techniques like sentiment analysis or fact-checking to
ensure that the generated text is objective and factually
accurate.

Deal With The Problem Of Generating Text That Is
Too Literal Or Lacks Nuance :
Use techniques like irony detection or sarcasm detection to
ensure that the generated text is nuanced and contextually
appropriate.

Handle The Problem Of Generating Text That Is Too Imprecise
Or Lacks Specificity :
Use techniques like fine-tuning or custom training to ensure
that the generated text is precise and specific to the task at
hand.

Avoid Generating Text That Is Too Dependent On
The Language Or Writing Style Of The Training Data
Use techniques like cross-lingual or cross-domain transfer
learning to ensure that the generated text can adapt to
different languages and writing styles.

Ethical Considerations in Using A.I. NLP Prompt Practitioner

Here are some ethical considerations in using A.I. NLP Prompt Practitioner

Privacy Text generated by language models can contain sensitive information about individuals. It is important to ensure that privacy is protected, and that any sensitive information is not released or shared without explicit consent.

Misinformation Text generated by language models can be used to spread misinformation and propaganda. It is important to ensure that generated text is factually accurate and not used to spread false information.

Ownership and Attribution Text generated by language models can be considered intellectual property. It is important to ensure that ownership and attribution are clearly defined and that any generated text is not used without appropriate permissions or attributions.

Harmful Content Text generated by language models can be used to generate harmful content such as hate speech, harassment, and threats. It is important to implement techniques to detect and prevent the generation of such content.

Transparency The algorithms and models used in text generation can be complex and difficult to understand. It is important to ensure that the process and decisions made by the language model are transparent and explainable to ensure accountability and ethical use.

Informed Consent If generated text is being used in research or commercial applications, it is important to ensure that individuals providing the data or consuming the generated text have provided informed consent and understand the potential uses and implications of the text generation.

Regulation and Oversight Text generation technologies can have significant social and ethical implications. It may be necessary to implement regulatory frameworks and oversight mechanisms to ensure that language models are used ethically and responsibly.

Accountability Language models can be used to generate text at scale, making it difficult to identify and address unethical behavior. It is important to ensure that there is accountability for the use of generated text and that appropriate measures are in place to prevent unethical behavior.

CHAPTER 7
AI. N.L.P. PROMPT PRACTITIONER
FUTURE DEVELOPMENTS

Here are some potential future developments for the A.I. N.L.P.
Prompt Practitioner:

Enhanced Control:
Future developments may allow users to have more control
over the generated text. This could include the ability to specify
certain characteristics such as tone, style, or length.

Improved Naturalness:
Language models may continue to improve in their ability to
generate natural-sounding text that is indistinguishable from
human-written content.

Multi-modal Generation:
Future developments may allow for the generation of not only
text, but also other modalities such as images, video, and audio,
resulting in more immersive and engaging content.

Personalization:
Language models may become more capable of generating text
that is tailored to individual preferences and needs, providing a
more personalized user experience.

Zero-shot Learning:
Language models may become more capable of generating
text in languages and domains for which they have not been
explicitly trained, through techniques such as zero-shot
learning.

Continued Expansion:
The size and complexity of language models are likely to continue to increase, enabling them to generate more diverse and complex text.

Transfer Learning:
Future developments may enable language models to transfer knowledge learned from one task or domain to another, leading to more efficient and effective text generation.

Human-in-the-Loop:
Future developments may incorporate more human oversight and feedback into the text generation process, allowing for greater control and guidance.

Interpretable Models:
As language models become more complex, it may become more important to develop techniques for interpreting their internal workings and decision-making processes.

Collaborative Generation:
Future developments may allow for multiple language models or users to collaborate in the generation of text, leading to more diverse and creative outputs.

Better Incorporation of Knowledge:
Language models may become more capable of incorporating structured knowledge and domain-specific information into the generation process, resulting in more accurate and informative text.

Emotion and Sentiment:
Future developments may enable language models to generate text that accurately conveys emotions and sentiment, opening up new applications in areas such as customer service and mental health.

Cognitive Computing:
Language models may become more integrated with other
cognitive computing technologies such as natural language
understanding and reasoning, resulting in more sophisticated
text generation capabilities.

Creative Generation:
Future developments may enable language models to
generate text that is not just informative, but also creative
and imaginative, leading to new applications in areas such as
advertising and content creation.

Explainable AI:
As language models become more complex and powerful,
it may become more important to develop techniques for
explaining their outputs and decision-making processes to
users.

Multilingual Generation:
Future developments may enable language models to generate
text in multiple languages, with a high level of accuracy and
fluency, opening up new opportunities in global communication
and translation.

Domain-Specific Models:
Language models may become more specialized for specific
domains, such as medicine or law, enabling more accurate and
informative text generation in those areas.

Contextual Adaptation:
 developments may enable language models to adapt
to different contextual cues, such as user preferences or
situational factors, resulting in more personalized and relevant
text generation.

More Efficient Models:
As language models become larger and more complex, there may be a growing need for more efficient models that can generate high-quality text with fewer computational resources.

Cross-Modal Generation:
Future developments may enable language models to generate text that is closely integrated with other modalities such as images or video, resulting in more immersive and engaging content.

Controllable Generation:
 Future developments may enable users to have more control over the generation process, allowing them to specify certain constraints or requirements for the generated text.

Improved Diversity:
As language models become more sophisticated, there may be an increased emphasis on generating diverse and varied text that avoids repetitive or biased output.

Collaborative Generation:
Future developments may enable multiple language models to work together to generate more complex and nuanced text, such as in collaborative writing or translation.

Cross-Lingual Generation:
 Language models may become more adept at generating text that seamlessly combines multiple languages, opening up new possibilities for multilingual communication and content creation.

Personalization:
Future developments may enable language models to generate
text that is personalized to individual users, taking into account
their preferences and previous interactions with the model.

Privacy and Security:
As language models become more widely used, there may
be a growing need to address issues of privacy and security,
such as ensuring that sensitive information is not inadvertently
generated or leaked.

Real-Time Generation:
Future developments may enable language models to generate
text in real-time, such as in chatbots or voice assistants,
resulting in more seamless and natural interactions with users.

Multimodal Input:
Language models may become more adept at processing and
generating text from multiple input modalities, such as images
or audio, resulting in more integrated and immersive content.

Explainable Generation:
As language models become more complex, there may be a
growing need for techniques that help users understand how
the generated text was produced, such as through the use of
visualizations or explanations.

Continual Learning:
Future developments may enable language models to learn and
adapt over time, allowing them to continually improve their
performance and accuracy even in changing environments.

Emerging Trends and Technologies
in Text Generation

Here is some information on emerging trends and technologies in text generation:

GPT-3 and Beyond:
OpenAI's GPT-3 model has set a new benchmark for language models, and researchers are working on even more advanced models that can generate even more complex and nuanced text.

Transformer Architectures:
Transformer architectures have become a dominant paradigm in natural language processing, and new transformer-based models are being developed for text generation tasks.

Zero-Shot Learning:
Zero-shot learning techniques enable language models to generate text in languages or domains that they haven't been explicitly trained on, which could lead to more diverse and versatile language models.

Federated Learning:
Federated learning is a technique that allows multiple devices to contribute to the training of a central model without sharing their data, which could enable the development of more privacy-preserving language models.

Few-Shot Learning:
Few-shot learning is a technique that enables language models to learn from just a few examples, which could enable the development of more adaptable and flexible language models.

Multi-Task Learning:
Multi-task learning enables language models to simultaneously learn multiple related tasks, such as text generation and summarization, which could lead to more efficient and versatile language models.

Generative Adversarial Networks (GANs):
GANs are a type of neural network that can generate realistic and diverse text, and researchers are exploring their potential for text generation tasks.

Knowledge Graphs:
Knowledge graphs are a structured representation of knowledge, and researchers are exploring how they can be used to improve the accuracy and coherence of generated text.

Explainable AI:
Explainable AI techniques enable users to understand how a language model is generating text, which could be important for ensuring transparency and accountability in text generation.

Quantum Computing:
Quantum computing is a rapidly advancing technology that could enable the development of more powerful and efficient language models, although the practical implications for text generation are still unclear.

Meta-Learning:
Meta-learning techniques enable language models to learn how to learn, which could lead to more efficient and adaptable models.

Reinforcement Learning:
Reinforcement learning techniques enable language models to learn from feedback, which could lead to more personalized and responsive text generation.

Neuro-Symbolic AI:
Neuro-symbolic AI is an emerging field that combines symbolic reasoning and deep learning, and researchers are exploring its potential for text generation tasks.

Contextual Embeddings:
Contextual embeddings enable language models to better capture the context of a piece of text, which could lead to more accurate and coherent generated text.

Self-Supervised Learning:
Self-supervised learning techniques enable language models to learn from unlabeled data, which could lead to more efficient and data-efficient models.

Continual Learning:
Continual learning techniques enable language models to continuously learn from new data without forgetting what they've already learned, which could lead to more adaptable and lifelong learning models.

Interpretable Models:
Interpretable models enable users to understand how a language model is generating text, which could be important for ensuring transparency and accountability in text generation.

Transfer Learning:
Transfer learning techniques enable language models to transfer knowledge learned from one task to another, which could lead to more data-efficient and versatile models.

Multimodal Text Generation:
Multimodal text generation is an emerging field that combines text with other modalities such as images, video, and audio, which could lead to more expressive and engaging generated text.

Human-in-the-Loop:
Human-in-the-loop techniques enable human feedback to be incorporated into the training and generation process of language models, which could lead to more personalized and user-friendly text generation.

Future Directions and Possibilities for ChatGPT Prompt Practitioner

ChatGPT has already shown immense potential in various fields such as natural language processing, chatbot development, content generation, and more. However, there are still many future directions and possibilities for ChatGPT prompt practitioners to explore.

Here are a few of them:

Multilingual Support:
While ChatGPT already supports multiple languages, there is still room for improvement in terms of accuracy and fluency. Future developments in this area could involve training the model on more diverse data sets and fine-tuning its parameters to better handle different languages' nuances.

Personalization:
ChatGPT could be further customized to better understand individual users' preferences and respond accordingly. This could involve incorporating user data from different sources, such as social media or browsing history, to create a more tailored experience.

Emotional Intelligence:
As AI models become more advanced, there is a growing interest in developing emotional intelligence for chatbots. ChatGPT could be trained to recognize and respond to different emotions, such as frustration, sadness, or excitement, to create a more empathetic interaction with users.

Creative Writing:
ChatGPT has already demonstrated its ability to generate coherent and engaging text, but future developments could focus on harnessing its creative potential. ChatGPT could be trained to generate poetry, fiction, or even screenplays, opening up new possibilities for content creation.

Expert Systems:
ChatGPT could be used to develop expert systems in various fields, such as medicine, law, or finance. By training the model on domain-specific data, it could provide insights and recommendations to users seeking advice in those fields.

Contextual Understanding:
ChatGPT could be further developed to better understand the context of a conversation and respond accordingly. This could involve incorporating more contextual information, such as user location or time of day, to create a more personalized and relevant experience.

Natural Language Understanding:
ChatGPT could be trained to better understand the nuances of human language, including idioms, slang, and regional dialects. This would improve the model's ability to communicate with users in a more natural and authentic way.

Interactive Learning:
ChatGPT could be trained to learn from user feedback and adapt its responses accordingly. This would create a more dynamic and interactive conversation between the user and the model.

Ethics And Bias:
As AI becomes more integrated into society, there is a growing concern about the ethics and biases that may be embedded in these systems. ChatGPT prompt practitioners could focus on developing ethical and unbiased models that are transparent and accountable.

Augmented Reality:
ChatGPT could be integrated with augmented reality technology to create more immersive and interactive experiences for users. This could involve using chatbots to provide information and guidance in real-time, as users navigate a physical space.

Sentiment Analysis:
ChatGPT could be trained to analyze the sentiment of a conversation and respond accordingly. This would allow the model to adapt its tone and language to better match the user's emotional state.

Personal Assistants:
ChatGPT could be developed into a personal assistant, capable of performing tasks such as scheduling appointments, setting reminders, and making reservations.

Customer Service:
ChatGPT could be used in customer service settings, providing users with fast and efficient support for common queries and issues.

Collaboration:
ChatGPT could be used to facilitate collaboration between users in different locations or time zones. This could involve creating virtual meeting rooms where users can chat with each other and with the model to coordinate tasks and projects.

Education:
ChatGPT could be used in education settings, providing students with personalized feedback and guidance on assignments and coursework. It could also be used to create interactive and engaging educational content.

Generative Art:
ChatGPT could be trained to generate artistic content, such as images, videos, and music. This could enable new forms of creative expression and help automate certain aspects of the creative process.

News And Journalism:
ChatGPT could be used to generate news articles and other journalistic content. This could help improve the speed and accuracy of news reporting and create more personalized and relevant news feeds for users.

Health And Wellness:
ChatGPT could be used in health and wellness settings, providing users with personalized health recommendations and advice. It could also be used to provide emotional support and counseling.

Gaming:
ChatGPT could be used to create interactive and engaging games, either as a game master or as a virtual player. This could create new forms of gameplay and enhance the gaming experience for users.

Storytelling:
ChatGPT could be used to create immersive and interactive storytelling experiences, either as a virtual narrator or as a participant in the story. This could enable new forms of storytelling and entertainment.

Marketing And Advertising:
ChatGPT could be used in marketing and advertising settings, providing personalized recommendations and offers to users. It could also be used to create more engaging and interactive ads.

E-Commerce:
ChatGPT could be used in e-commerce settings, helping users find and purchase products that match their preferences and needs. It could also be used to provide customer support and address common issues.

Virtual Assistants:
ChatGPT could be integrated into virtual assistants, such as Amazon's Alexa or Google Assistant. This could enable users to interact with these assistants in a more natural and conversational way.

Translation And Interpretation:
ChatGPT could be used to improve the accuracy and fluency of machine translation and interpretation systems. This could help break down language barriers and enable more effective communication between people who speak different languages.

Robotics:
ChatGPT could be used to enable more natural and intuitive interactions between humans and robots. This could help make robots more user-friendly and improve their ability to assist and interact with humans.

Legal:
ChatGPT could be used to assist with legal tasks, such as drafting contracts or providing legal advice. This could help make legal services more accessible and affordable for individuals and small businesses.

Social Media:
ChatGPT could be used to enhance social media experiences, by providing personalized recommendations, facilitating conversations, and helping users navigate complex social networks.

Autonomous Vehicles:
ChatGPT could be used to enable more natural and intuitive interactions between passengers and autonomous vehicles. This could help make the experience of riding in a self-driving car more comfortable and enjoyable.

Mental Health:
ChatGPT could be used to provide mental health support and counseling, by offering personalized advice and resources to individuals struggling with mental health issues.

Disaster Response:
ChatGPT could be used to assist with disaster response efforts, by providing information and guidance to individuals affected by natural disasters or other emergencies.

Music:
ChatGPT could be used to generate music, either as a composer or as a collaborator with human musicians. This could enable new forms of musical expression and help automate certain aspects of the music-making process.

Sports:
ChatGPT could be used to provide real-time commentary and analysis for sports events, or to assist coaches and players with game strategy and training.

Politics And Governance:
ChatGPT could be used to engage citizens in political and governance processes, by providing personalized information and facilitating conversations with elected officials.

Agriculture:
ChatGPT could be used to provide personalized advice and guidance to farmers, helping them make more informed decisions about planting, harvesting, and managing their crops.

Energy And Utilities:

ChatGPT could be used to assist with energy and utilities management, by providing personalized recommendations for energy efficiency and conservation, or by helping users navigate complex billing and payment systems.

Aviation:

ChatGPT could be used to provide real-time flight information and personalized recommendations to air travelers, or to assist pilots with flight planning and navigation.

Education:

ChatGPT could be used to provide personalized education and training, by offering individualized lesson plans and feedback to students.

Real Estate:

ChatGPT could be used to provide personalized recommendations and guidance to individuals looking to buy or sell real estate, helping them find properties that match their preferences and needs.

Finance:

ChatGPT could be used to provide personalized financial advice and recommendations, helping individuals make informed decisions about investments, savings, and other financial matters.

Tourism:

ChatGPT could be used to provide personalized recommendations and information to travelers, helping them plan and book trips that match their preferences and interests.

Fashion And Beauty:

ChatGPT could be used to provide personalized fashion and beauty advice, helping individuals find clothes and cosmetics that match their preferences and needs.

Environmental Sustainability:
ChatGPT could be used to provide personalized recommendations for environmental sustainability, helping individuals and businesses reduce their carbon footprint and adopt more sustainable practices.

Human Resources:
ChatGPT could be used to assist with human resources management, by providing personalized advice and guidance to employees and managers.

Healthcare Research:
ChatGPT could be used to assist with healthcare research, by generating hypotheses and conducting data analysis to identify new treatments and cures for diseases.

Space Exploration:
ChatGPT could be used to assist with space exploration, by providing real-time information and analysis to astronauts and ground crews, or by generating hypotheses for new space missions and discoveries.

Gaming:
ChatGPT could be used to enhance gaming experiences, by providing personalized recommendations and gameplay strategies, or by generating new game concepts.

Customer service:
ChatGPT could be used to provide personalized customer service, by assisting with common inquiries, resolving issues, and providing product information.

Journalism:
ChatGPT could be used to assist with journalism, by providing personalized news and analysis, or by generating article ideas and drafts.

Cybersecurity:
ChatGPT could be used to assist with cybersecurity, by identifying and addressing potential security risks and threats in real-time.

Transportation And Logistics:
ChatGPT could be used to optimize transportation and logistics, by providing real-time recommendations for route planning and inventory management.

The possibilities for ChatGPT prompt practitioners are vast and constantly expanding as the technology continues to evolve.

As AI becomes more integrated into our daily lives, it is likely that ChatGPT will play an increasingly significant role in shaping the way we interact with technology and each other.

APPENDIX A
GLOSSARY OF KEY TERMS
USED IN THE TEXTBOOK

Artificial Intelligence (AI): The simulation of human intelligence processes by machines, especially computer systems.

Chatbot: A computer program designed to simulate conversation with human users, especially over the internet.

Deep Learning: A subset of machine learning in which artificial neural networks, algorithms inspired by the human brain, learn from large amounts of data.

Dialogue System: A computer system designed to engage in natural language conversations with human users.

Generative Pre-trained Transformer (GPT): A type of deep learning model that uses unsupervised learning to pre-train a language model, which can then be fine-tuned for specific natural language processing tasks.

Language Modeling: A type of natural language processing task that involves predicting the next word or sequence of words in a sentence or text.

Machine Learning (ML): A type of artificial intelligence that allows computer systems to automatically improve their performance with experience.

Natural Language Processing (NLP): A subfield of artificial intelligence that focuses on enabling computers to understand, interpret, and generate human language.

OpenAI: An artificial intelligence research laboratory consisting of the for-profit corporation OpenAI LP and its parent company, the non-profit OpenAI Inc.

Prompt: A short phrase or sentence provided as input to a natural language processing system to initiate a conversation or generate a response.

Transfer Learning: A machine learning technique that involves leveraging knowledge learned from one task to improve performance on a related but different task.

Attention Mechanism: A mechanism used in deep learning models to focus on certain parts of input when making predictions or generating output.

Bidirectional Encoder Representations from Transformers (BERT): A pre-trained deep learning model for natural language processing that uses bidirectional training and context awareness to achieve state-of-the-art performance on a wide range of NLP tasks.

Conditional Generation: A type of generative modeling that involves generating output based on a given input or condition.

Contextualized Word Embeddings: A type of word embedding that takes into account the context in which a word appears, allowing for more accurate and nuanced representations of word meaning.

Domain Adaptation: A machine learning technique that involves training a model on one domain and adapting it to work well on a different domain.

Fine-tuning: A technique in transfer learning where a pre-trained model is further trained on a specific task or domain, often with a small amount of task-specific data.

Hyperparameters: Parameters in a machine learning model that are not learned from the data, but instead must be set by the user or optimized through trial and error.

Language Generation: A type of natural language processing task that involves generating human-like language, such as sentences, paragraphs, or stories.

Masked Language Modeling: A type of language modeling task that involves predicting a missing word in a sentence or text.

Multi-task Learning: A machine learning technique that involves training a model to perform multiple related tasks simultaneously.

Natural Language Understanding (NLU): A subfield of NLP that focuses on the ability of computers to understand the meaning of human language.

Natural Language Generation (NLG): A subfield of NLP that focuses on the ability of computers to generate human-like language.

Overfitting: A phenomenon in machine learning where a model becomes too complex and starts to fit the noise in the training data instead of the underlying patterns, leading to poor generalization performance.

Pre-Processing: The process of preparing raw data for use in a machine learning model, which often involves cleaning, transforming, and encoding the data.

Recurrent Neural Network (RNN): A type of neural network that can process sequential data, such as language or time series, by maintaining a hidden state that depends on previous inputs.

Sampling: A technique used in generative modeling to generate output by randomly selecting from a set of possible options.

Self-Attention: An attention mechanism used in some deep learning models that allows the model to attend to different parts of its own input when making predictions or generating output.

Semi-Supervised Learning: A machine learning technique that involves training a model with both labeled and unlabeled data, which can help improve performance when labeled data is scarce.

Transformer: A type of deep learning model for natural language processing that uses self-attention and multi-head attention to capture long-range dependencies and relationships between words or tokens.

Adversarial Training: A technique used in machine learning to train models to be more robust to adversarial examples, which are inputs that have been intentionally modified to mislead the model.

Attention Score: A value used in attention mechanisms to determine the importance of different parts of input when making predictions or generating output.

Beam Search: A search algorithm used in natural language generation to generate output by considering multiple candidate sequences in parallel and selecting the most likely sequence based on a scoring function.

Encoder-Decoder Architecture: A type of deep learning architecture used in natural language processing that involves an encoder network that converts input into a fixed-length representation, and a decoder network that generates output based on the encoded representation.

Evaluation Metric: A metric used to evaluate the performance of a machine learning model on a specific task, such as accuracy, precision, recall, or F1 score.

One-Shot Learning: A machine learning technique that involves training a model to learn from a single or a few examples, which can help improve performance when labeled data is scarce.

Perplexity: A measure of how well a language model can predict a sequence of words, calculated as the exponentiated average negative log-likelihood of each word in the sequence.

Reinforcement Learning: A type of machine learning that involves training a model to make decisions based on rewards and punishments received in response to its actions.

Sequence-to-Sequence (Seq2Seq) Model: A type of deep learning model used in natural language processing that involves an encoder network that converts input into a fixed-length representation, and a decoder network that generates output based on the encoded representation.

Transformer-XL: A variant of the Transformer model for natural language processing that uses segment-level recurrence and relative positional encoding to capture longer-term dependencies between words or tokens.

Anchor Text: The visible, clickable text in a hyperlink, which provides context and tells search engines what the linked page is about.

Bag-of-Words Model: A simple natural language processing model that represents a document as a set of its words, without considering their order or context.

Content-based Filtering: A recommendation system technique that recommends items to a user based on the content of items the user has interacted with previously.

Data Augmentation: A technique used to increase the amount of training data for machine learning models by artificially creating new examples through techniques such as flipping, rotating, or cropping images, or adding noise or distortion to audio or text data.

Dropout: A regularization technique used in machine learning to prevent overfitting by randomly dropping out some of the neurons during training.

Federated Learning: A machine learning technique that involves training models on decentralized devices, such as smartphones, and aggregating the updates to the central model, rather than collecting all the data in a central location.

Gradient Descent: An optimization algorithm used in machine learning to minimize the loss function of a model by iteratively adjusting the model's parameters in the direction of the steepest descent of the gradient.

Hyperparameter: A parameter that controls the behavior of a machine learning algorithm, such as the learning rate, regularization strength, or number of layers in a neural network, and must be set prior to training the model.

Imbalanced Data: A situation where the distribution of classes in a dataset is highly uneven, with one or a few classes having much fewer examples than the others.

Inference: The process of using a trained machine learning model to make predictions on new, unseen data.

Latent Space: A low-dimensional space in which high-dimensional data can be represented in a more compact and meaningful form, often used in dimensionality reduction or generative models.

Multi-Armed Bandit: A problem in decision theory that involves choosing between multiple options with uncertain rewards, where the goal is to maximize the total reward over time.

Overfitting: A situation where a machine learning model fits the training data too closely and performs poorly on new, unseen data due to capturing noise or irrelevant patterns in the data.

Random Forest: A machine learning algorithm that combines multiple decision trees trained on subsets of the data and features, and uses their aggregate output to make predictions.

Regularization: A technique used in machine learning to prevent overfitting by adding a penalty term to the loss function that discourages large weights or complex models.

Stochastic Gradient Descent: A variant of gradient descent that uses a randomly selected subset of the training data, or mini-batch, to estimate the gradient and update the parameters, which can accelerate the training process.

Tensor: A multi-dimensional array used to represent data in deep learning models, such as images, audio signals, or text sequences.

Transfer Learning: A machine learning technique that involves using a pre-trained model as a starting point for a new task, and fine-tuning its parameters on a smaller dataset.

Variational Autoencoder: A type of generative model that uses a neural network to learn a low-dimensional representation of data that can be used to generate new, similar data.

Zero-Shot Learning: A machine learning technique that involves training a model to recognize new classes that were not present in the training data, by leveraging prior knowledge or semantic relationships between classes.

APPENDIX B: REFERENCES

Goodfellow, I., Bengio, Y., & Courville, A. (2016). Deep Learning. MIT Press.

Jurafsky, D., & Martin, J. H. (2019). Speech and Language Processing. Pearson Education.

Manning, C. D., & Schütze, H. (1999). Foundations of Statistical Natural Language Processing. MIT Press.

Ng, A. (2017). Machine Learning Yearning. Andrew Ng.

Russel, S. J., & Norvig, P. (2010). Artificial Intelligence: A Modern Approach. Prentice Hall.

Shalev-Shwartz, S., & Ben-David, S. (2014). Understanding Machine Learning: From Theory to Algorithms. Cambridge University Press.

Silver, D., Huang, A., Maddison, C. J., Guez, A., Sifre, L., Van Den Driessche, G., ... & Hassabis, D. (2016). Mastering the game of Go with deep neural networks and tree search. Nature, 529(7587), 484-489.

Sutton, R. S., & Barto, A. G. (2018). Reinforcement Learning: An Introduction. MIT Press.

Vaswani, A., Shazeer, N., Parmar, N., Uszkoreit, J., Jones, L., Gomez, A. N., ... & Polosukhin, I. (2017). Attention is all you need. In Advances in Neural Information Processing Systems (pp. 5998-6008).

Zhang, C., Bengio, S., Hardt, M., Recht, B., & Vinyals, O. (2017). Understanding deep learning requires rethinking generalization. arXiv preprint arXiv:1611.03530.

Abadi, M., Barham, P., Chen, J., Chen, Z., Davis, A., Dean, J., ... & Zheng, X. (2016). TensorFlow: A system for large-scale machine learning. In 12th USENIX Symposium on Operating Systems Design and Implementation (OSDI 16) (pp. 265-283).

Bahdanau, D., Cho, K., & Bengio, Y. (2015). Neural machine translation by jointly learning to align and translate. In Proceedings of the International Conference on Learning Representations (ICLR).

Collobert, R., Weston, J., Bottou, L., Karlen, M., Kavukcuoglu, K., & Kuksa, P. (2011). Natural language processing (almost) from scratch. Journal of Machine Learning Research, 12, 2493-2537.

Devlin, J., Chang, M. W., Lee, K., & Toutanova, K. (2018). BERT: Pre-training of deep bidirectional transformers for language understanding. In Proceedings of the Annual Conference of the North American Chapter of the Association for Computational Linguistics (NAACL-HLT).

Hinton, G., Deng, L., Yu, D., Dahl, G. E., Mohamed, A. R., Jaitly, N., ... & Kingsbury, B. (2012). Deep neural networks for acoustic modeling in speech recognition: The shared views of four research groups. IEEE Signal Processing Magazine, 29(6), 82-97.

Hochreiter, S., & Schmidhuber, J. (1997). Long short-term memory. Neural Computation, 9(8), 1735-1780.

LeCun, Y., Bengio, Y., & Hinton, G. (2015). Deep learning. Nature, 521(7553), 436-444.

Mikolov, T., Chen, K., Corrado, G., & Dean, J. (2013). Efficient estimation of word representations in vector space. In Proceedings of the International Conference on Learning Representations (ICLR).

Mnih, V., Kavukcuoglu, K., Silver, D., Rusu, A. A., Veness, J., Bellemare, M. G., ... & Petersen, S. (2015). Human-level control through deep reinforcement learning. Nature, 518(7540), 529-533.

Papineni, K., Roukos, S., Ward, T., & Zhu, W. J. (2002). BLEU: A method for automatic evaluation of machine translation. In Proceedings of the Annual Meeting of the Association for Computational Linguistics (ACL).

Pennington, J., Socher, R., & Manning, C. (2014). GloVe: Global vectors for word representation. In Proceedings of the Conference on Empirical Methods in Natural Language Processing (EMNLP).

Radford, A., Narasimhan, K., Salimans, T., & Sutskever, I. (2018). Improving language understanding with unsupervised learning. Technical Report, OpenAI.

Ruder, S. (2017). An overview of multi-task learning in deep neural networks. arXiv preprint arXiv:1706.05098.

Vaswani, A., Shazeer, N., Parmar, N., Uszkoreit, J., Jones, L., Gomez, A. N., ... & Polosukhin, I. (2017). Attention is all you need. In Proceedings of the Conference on Neural Information Processing Systems (NeurIPS).

Weng, L., Lu, J., & Yang, Q. (2018). A survey on transfer learning. IEEE Transactions on Knowledge and Data Engineering, 29(10), 2258-2285.

Wu, Y., Schuster, M., Chen, Z., Le, Q. V., Norouzi, M., Macherey, W., ... & Adams, R. P. (2016). Google's neural machine translation system: Bridging the gap between human and machine translation. arXiv preprint arXiv:1609.08144.

Yang, Z., Dai, Z., Yang, Y., Carbonell, J. G., Salakhutdinov, R., & Le, Q. V. (2019). XLNet: Generalized autoregressive pretraining for language understanding. In Proceedings of the Conference on Neural Information Processing Systems (NeurIPS).

Zhang, Y., Sun, Y., Jin, H., & Ye, J. (2018). Deep learning for multi-task learning: A review. arXiv preprint arXiv:1706.05098.

Zoph, B., & Le, Q. V. (2017). Neural architecture search with reinforcement learning. In Proceedings of the Conference on Computer Vision and Pattern Recognition (CVPR).

Dai, Z., Yang, Z., Yang, Y., Carbonell, J. G., Salakhutdinov, R., & Le, Q. V. (2019). Transformer-XL: Attentive language models beyond a fixed-length context. In Proceedings of the Conference on Empirical Methods in Natural Language Processing (EMNLP).

Howard, J., & Ruder, S. (2018). Universal language model fine-tuning for text classification. In Proceedings of the Conference on Empirical Methods in Natural Language Processing (EMNLP).

Radford, A., Wu, J., Child, R., Luan, D., Amodei, D., & Sutskever, I. (2019). Language models are unsupervised multitask learners. Technical Report, OpenAI.

Liu, Y., Ott, M., Goyal, N., Du, J., Joshi, M., Chen, D., ... & Stoyanov, V. (2019). RoBERTa: A robustly optimized BERT pretraining approach. arXiv preprint arXiv:1907.11692.

www.ingramcontent.com/pod-product-compliance
Lightning Source LLC
Chambersburg PA
CBHW080027260726
48658CB00007B/2506